Children and Media Outside the Home

Children and Media Outside the Home

Playing and Learning in After-School Care

Karen Orr Vered

First published 2008 by
PALGRAVE MACMILLAN
Houndmills, Basingstoke, Hampshire RG21 6XS and
175 Fifth Avenue, New York, N.Y. 10010
Companies and representatives throughout the world

PALGRAVE MACMILLAN is the global academic imprint of the Palgrave Macmillan division of St. Martin's Press, LLC and of Palgrave Macmillan Ltd. Macmillan® is a registered trademark in the United States, United Kingdom and other countries. Palgrave is a registered trademark in the European Union and other countries.

ISBN-13: 978-0-230-53729-3   hardback
iSBN-10: 0-230-53729-4   hardback

This book is printed on paper suitable for recycling and made from fully managed and sustained forest sources. Logging, pulping and manufacturing processes are expected to conform to the environmental regulations of the country of origin.

A catalogue record for this book is available from the British Library.

A catalog record for this book is available from the Library of Congress.

10   9   8   7   6   5   4   3   2   1
17 16 15 14 13 12 11 10 09 08

Printed and bound in Great Britain by
CPI Antony Rowe, Chippenham and Eastbourne

Contents

Figures

Acknowledgements

I have to thank many supporters, colleagues, and friends who helped me in shaping and conducting the research and writing this book. This project would not have been realized without the support and assistance of the Department of Education and Children's Services (DECS) in South Australia, most especially Suzy McKenna who helped initiate the research when she was a Manager for Out of School Hours Care (OSHC). Equally important, the OSHC Association of South Australia extended financial assistance to the project at a critical juncture and their generosity was later complemented by a grant from the DECS. Flinders University also supported the project financially and by granting me study leave.

I wish to particularly thank my colleagues in Screen Studies at Flinders University for their encouragement, especially Richard Maltby, who has always been willing to have a serious discussion about play. And thanks also to old friends and new, Marsha Kinder, who continues to be an inspiration for my professional life; David Buckingham, who has been supportive of my research activities; and Victoria Haskins, who provides a critical eye and judicious application of red ink for most of my work. The research assistance provided by Aanya Roenfeldt and Danny Wattin, who conducted half of the site observations and interviews, was invaluable. Thank-you to Bowen Ellames, who sketched the drawings for the book, based on photographs taken during research. Thanks also to the OSHC services, their staff, and the children who participated in this study; the book would not have been possible without their cooperation. I hope that this book fairly and thoroughly represents the intricacies of media play in OSHC. And finally, a thank-you to the helpful staff at Palgrave who oversaw publication: Melanie Blair, Jill Lake, and Christabel Scaife. Any errors in this work are solely my responsibility.

I dedicate this book, my first, to the memory of my mother, whose talent with children and commitment to the profession of teaching continue to guide me. And to my father, who, when I announced at age 12 that I wanted to be a lawyer, said, 'Lawyer hell, you can be a judge!' The encouragement, guidance, and support my parents have given me throughout my lifetime shares in the credit for all of my achievements.

Introduction

Imagine you're responsible for the holiday entertainment and recreation of 70 primary school children between the ages of 5 and 12. It's two weeks before school lets out for the summer holiday and you've advertised your programme, including an excursion to the sure-to-be-hit film *Harry Potter and the Philosopher's Stone*. And then, to your complete surprise, you're told you cannot take the children to see this film because it's 'rated PG.' *Harry Potter* requires Parental Guidance. On the verge of the summer holidays, one Director for a Vacation Care service had precisely this experience.

I heard this story in late November 2001, three days before the movie opened in South Australia. I was delivering the last half of a two-part workshop about children's leisure-time media use. Nine Directors of Out of School Hours Care (OSHC) services and one representative of the training organization that had contracted me were participating. As they arrived and exchanged 'hellos,' their conversation quickly turned to a challenging discussion of how film classification (ratings) impacts OSHC services during the school holidays. For a moment, I flattered myself by thinking that the workshop content had spurred this discussion. Once I was brought up to speed, I understood that real events, not hypothetical ones presented in the workshop, were behind this lively debate and reflection. What happened?

A school principal told the Director of the Vacation Care programme, which operates on the school grounds, that the children were not to be taken to see *Harry Potter and the Philosopher's Stone*. This decision was made because the film carried a PG classification from the Office of Film and Literature Classification (OFLC), the body responsible for classification of film, video, literature, and electronic games in Australia.[1] The school principal asserted that educational guidelines within the Department of

Education plainly excluded screening PG-classified films to children in the 5- to 12-year-old age bracket. Since OSHC services and Vacation Care services (school holiday care for school-aged children) fall under the auspices of the School Council when operated on school grounds, the School Principal, as head of that council, has the right to assert authority over service operation, although this is quite uncommon.

Listening to their informal discussion, I gathered that the workshop participants were simultaneously pleased and worried by the *Harry Potter* ban. They were anxious because they feared that a similar ban might be imposed on their OSHC services, when they were all counting on *Harry Potter and the Philosopher's Stone* to be a highly popular, perhaps even repeatable, excursion for the hot summer days ahead. They were, on the other hand, oddly pleased because the workshop was addressing precisely such issues and they were feeling empowered to defend the *Harry Potter* movie excursion, should they be challenged with a similar ban.

How is it possible that this film could be dismissed when the series of novels on which it is based is credited with increasing children's interest in reading for pleasure? To answer this question we need to understand the complex and often contradictory values, desires, and perceptions that regulate children's access to media. Examining this network of influences helps reveal how adults view children's media and children's media practices. What children actually do with media, however, is only structured in part by adult interventions and opinions. Children's culture, and specifically the ways in which they play with entertainment media, information communication technologies (ICT), and their associated story worlds also contribute to shaping children's media practices in the present, and probably for the future as well. Consequently, to understand how children acquire their media competency, we need to examine their media play as a form of activity that is indeed structured by adult regulation, but such regulation is only one influence in a much more complex ecology. By looking closely at children's everyday media play we can discover how it is structured and managed by both adults and peers. In the OSHC environment, it is useful to look at media in the context of play or as a play activity, alongside other activities. This view allows us to see how media play in recreational environments articulates with more serious uses of media in other arenas.

How *Harry Potter* came to be banned provides an interesting example of the complex ways in which popular entertainment media are positioned within, and negotiated through, the institutions that significantly shape young children's lives: families, schools, and childcare services. The film,

Harry Potter and the Philosopher's Stone, is situated precariously between school regulation and 'holiday fun.' In this instance, controversy over seeing the film points to the mediating role that OSHC continually serves between families and schools. Vacation Care was the site on which conflict was played out across formal regulations of schooling, children's attraction to and desire for popular entertainment, and the possibility of parental concern for a film that posed an outside chance of objection. The ban on *Harry Potter* in OSHC gives us an opportunity to recognize the importance of media in realms that are neither home nor classroom and to examine the relationships between media objects and their consumption.

This book presents an in-depth analysis of the place of media in children's leisure and the media practices they engage in at OSHC services so that we can gain a more thorough understanding of children's media culture, as it exists across the boundaries of home, classroom, and childcare institutions. It is an ethnographic study of young children between the ages of 5 and 12. This is the population on whose behalf most media regulation is enacted in Australia and elsewhere. As children grow older, they are often allowed greater independence with respect to media consumption and use, and this is reflected in media classification schemes and ratings such as MA15 (recommended for a Mature Audience over the age of 15).

Throughout this work, I have tried to present the rich detail of observation and stay true to not only the words but also the tone of children's remarks so that adult readers might gain an insight into children's views, knowledge, and feelings about their media practices. I have situated these accounts within a frame provided by the literature on children's media use and the many debates that structure research in this specialized area of media studies. It is my hope that by shedding light on the activities of OSHC, we will begin to recognize the importance of this place and learn how to capitalize on its unique qualities for the benefit of children and their continued pleasure with entertainment and information media.

My aim has been to write a book that can be read either in its entirety or in parts, in any sequence that serves the reader's interests. Chapter 1 explains why we need to look closely at media use in OSHC and how this study has taken steps to identify the informal media learning that can occur in OSHC.

Chapter 2 situates OSHC within a broader historical context along two dimensions. First, I review the history of childhood and childcare in Australia. The developmental history of OSHC is particularly important in Australia because the services are conceived as social services rather than educational services. This distinction has consequences for the positioning of entertainment media among other activities within OSHC and for the overall attitude towards media use as legitimate play. Secondly, philosophies about after-school care are compared with those in the US and UK because, while we share a common language and the Australian schooling system shares much with both the US and UK, OSHC in Australia is considerably different from what we find in the US and UK.

Chapter 3 explains the concept of intermediary space and argues that such spaces are important for children's informal acquisition of media competency. The intermediary nature of OSHC is discussed in terms of physical, temporal, and ideological dimensions. Descriptions of children's play styles and their own reflections on that play illustrate how time and space constraints and regulations shape their use of media in OSHC in ways that are quite different to what we see in homes and classrooms. Preliminary consideration of these ideas appeared in an essay published in *Simile* in 2001 (Vered, 2001).

Chapter 4 offers an example of how OSHC environments support particular ways of playing with media and follows with a discussion of associated forms of pleasure. Here too readers will find an explanation of official media regulation schemes operating within Australia. Chapter 5 looks closely at how children's leisure time is constructed and addresses the place of media play within the notion of 'productive play.'

Chapters 6 and 7 draw extensively upon the observation and interview data in their discussion of media provision, access, regulation, and play cultures in six services. TV and video playback are addressed in Chapter 6, while Chapter 7 looks closely at digital games and Internet use in OSHC.

Chapter 8 describes a movie-making programme offered by one of the OSHC services and demonstrates how children's fan and consumer practices inform their critical media competency. Chapter 9 brings the book to a close by summarizing how the research findings can be applied in practices that encourage children's informal learning and development of media competency.

1
Informal Learning and Media in After-School Care

> Children watch television as part of their social existence, and this is another dimension that cannot be ignored. In some respects the social dimension has not been neglected, because it is as a social problem that television has presented itself as demanding research.
>
> —Hodge & Tripp, 1986: 8

Since Hodge and Tripp first made their observation of television, children's access to media has increased exponentially. If they were writing their book today, the authors might include, among the media popularly characterized as posing a social problem, the newer media that children have adopted with enthusiasm: video and computer games, the Internet, personal technologies, and mobile media, such as phones. Over the past 20 years, the range of media platforms available to children has increased and this increase is complemented and complicated by the many locations in which children now have access to electronic media. It is no longer satisfactory to discuss children's media access as either 'at home' or 'at school.' Indeed, it may never have been sufficient to do so, but that is how the literature has constructed children's media use. This is perhaps a result of research efficiencies: researchers have had relatively easy access to study children in the confines of classrooms and sometimes they have also been able to research practices within homes. The increased diversity and proliferation of media now demand that we re-examine children's media use in light of the numerous changes that have taken place in technology, marketing, and children's lives, not least of which is increased mobility.

Hodge and Tripp took issue with the simplistic view of television as a 'social problem' and demonstrated how both children's lives and the place of television within them were complex. This book extends and updates that view by looking at one of the more recent complications in this mix: how children interact with media in Out of School Hours Care (OSHC), childcare for primary school children between the ages of 5 and 12.

In addition to homes and classrooms, young children now engage with entertainment and ICT in after-school programmes, camps, libraries, museums, kiosks, and in the back seat of the family car. Most studies about children's media practices still restrict investigation to the well-known and readily accessible contexts of home and classroom. They completely overlook the social dimension of entertainment media in other environments, and only recently have researchers undertaken to examine the growth of mobile and distributed technologies that are not fixed to specific physical locations, but which move with children, where ever they go.

To account for the social and cultural dimensions of media use in one of the places that is neither home nor classroom, but increasingly important to children's daily lives and their media practices, this book examines the complexity of children's media play in the intermediary space of after-school care. In Australia, OSHC for school-aged children (5- to 12-year-olds) is the fastest growing sector of the childcare industry; the number of services has more than quadrupled since 1989 (Department of Education, Training and Employment, 1999). OSHC is subsidized by the federal government as part of the overall provision of childcare. Importantly in Australia, such services are not conceived as social welfare services for a minority of struggling families but are, like Australian public health care provision, social services for all Australians. In South Australia, where the research for this book was conducted, OSHC services are most often provided on school grounds, and sometimes in community centres. Across the eight states and territories of Australia, there is some variation on this point and it is addressed more thoroughly in Chapter 2.

In 2003, the population of South Australia was a little more than 1.5 million. In total, 640 schools were classified as serving primary school children. There were 189 Registered Non-Government Primary schools (private schools). At this time there were 304 OSHC services in total and among them 216 were operating on school grounds, mostly in the public sector. Nearly one-third of the state-run primary schools offered after-school care services. Fee for OSHC services in South Australia ranges from $2.50 to $4.00 per hour, before a federal rebate that reduces the real cost further. (Detailed explanation of fee structures appears in Chapter 2.)

Most importantly for our purposes, electronic media in South Australian OSHC services share equal status with more traditional playthings and activities. That is to say, in OSHC services child's play with electronic media is considered legitimate leisure-time activity. This is quite different from what we would expect to find in the US or UK where, according to the literature, entertainment media is not a welcome part of the after-school care provision for young children.

This book takes the view that children's leisure-time use of media constitutes informal learning and as such their media play makes significant contributions to their overall knowledge of media. Studying children's media use in OSHC may enable us to understand how children's media play can support their formal learning and acquisition of skills with respect to ICT. I refer to this nexus of knowledge and skills as media competency.

When I began this study, I expected to find that OSHC in Australia would be quite similar to programmes in the US and UK. To my pleasant surprise, I have found that South Australian OSHC services take a more welcoming view of media play than reports indicate for the US and UK. Entertainment media, such as video games and television, are more common in South Australian OSHC than they are in similar US and UK services and programmes. To explain this fundamental difference, I have reviewed the history of childhood and childcare in Australia to trace the ways in which attitudes about children and childhood have informed how media are viewed in the larger context of children's leisure activities. The history of childcare in Australia is presented in Chapter 2.

While it is important to account for the new and different configurations among media platforms in children's lives, we must also take careful note of where and how media are socially situated (Giacquinta et al., 1993). Interestingly much of the concern over children's use of the Internet focuses on what occurs in private, not public, spaces. It is 'unsupervised' children who may cross boundaries and venture into the spaces of adult content. Unsupervised children may become innocent victims to the predatory deeds of unknown adults – the online version of 'stranger danger.' Unsupervised children are vulnerable. These concerns indicate, at heart, our fear that children and childhood are being corrupted by new media and by greater access to media overall. Although these fears have been popularly reported in the media for some time, and it is to be expected that crime would occur in the virtual world as it does elsewhere, Australian authorities did not maintain statistics about reports of online crimes against children until 2005.

Without such records it is impossible to verify the nature or scale of these occurrences with certainty. The rhetoric of stranger danger in the online world circulates freely and widely without much factual support to verify and characterize its presence. Nevertheless, as David Buckingham (2000) points out, adults will always try to control children's access to media; 'the question is not *whether* but *how* and *where* this takes place.' With respect to the Internet, children are often least supervised within their own homes.

Where and how regulation and censorship of media takes place is in part based on where media are placed and how they are used. That is to say, the social contexts in which media are found influence the ways in which we use the different technologies, how we characterize them, as beneficial or threatening, and the ways in which we manage hopes and fears about technologies. In the broadest terms, management is regulation. At a finer level, regulation may take the form of censorship as a particular management strategy. How children's access to and use of media technologies are regulated in OSHC is important for the differences that these configurations generate when compared with classroom and home management of media access and use. Experiences in all three places contribute to a child's overall media competency and, yet, they are very different experiences because they are very different places with unique regulatory systems.

Although the first wave of desktop computing occurred in the workplace, it was the second wave, associated with individual household adoption, which created an audience (consumer or user base) for many new media forms. As our interest in and dependence on these technologies and media forms has grown, we now find Internet kiosks in public spaces, and they are available on a pay-per-use basis like public phones. Coin-operated Internet access is available in most international airports, for example, and in the heavily touristed areas of large cities it is increasingly easy to find a range of Internet cafes and public user rooms that offer fee-based access. The latest generation of mobile phones is capable of delivering Internet access as well. Media that were once exclusive to the office desk or home study are now situated in cafes and airports, while more prestigious public use of media is facilitated by personal technologies, such as the mobile phone and personal digital assistants (PDA). Interestingly, as media move into the public sphere, a counter-momentum to privatize use is building once again, as we move away from the public access of a kiosk towards greater use of personal equivalents like PDAs.

For children, the increase in public access points for computer use may provide greater access for some and have little effect in the lives of the most privileged, those children who have computers at home. Certainly, equity in access is one of the reasons that governments and community agencies invest in equipping public access points, such as libraries, with computers and Internet connections. With respect to children's media and associated questions of regulation and management, the physical and social spaces where access occurs deserve critical attention. Once again, OSHC services are increasingly an important site for public access among primary school children in Australia.

Hodge and Tripp's groundbreaking study examined the reciprocal relationship between home culture and school culture and demonstrated how television was situated within and between each of those institutions. They argued that 'all television viewing is mediated to a greater or lesser extent by the family, the school and other factors, so that time accorded to viewing in the home is itself an aspect of culture' (1986: 173). Their study demonstrated how the culture of classrooms alternately valued and devalued television. That is, teachers and students sometimes ascribed cultural value to television as part of 'school learning' and at other times they denigrated or trivialized television. An important aspect of their work is that it highlights how culture shapes our ideological reception of media and how the meanings of media are shaped by the social contexts in which they are situated. That is to say that media do not have meaning independent of their social contexts and use. Meaning is ascribed to media, rather than fixed in either technology or content. This is why the PG classification of *Harry Potter and the Philosopher's Stone* became controversial. The meaning that a viewer would derive from the film would have to be understood in the wider context of its relationship to the book series and the rest of the franchise. The film's classification was thus at odds with the context of the larger franchise.

Children access media where they spend their time and, increasingly, they spend time outside the family home in a variety of settings, including childcare. OSHC is significant among media-rich environments and the ways in which media are used in OSHC reflect values that are derived in part from school culture and in part from home culture. Media use in OSHC is about learning and about leisure. This complicates the ways in which media access is controlled in OSHC because the *where* and *how* sometimes represent different systems of regulation.

Early twenty-first-century childhood and its associated media are creating new spaces for children's play. Collectively these new media and new play spaces are characterized by their intermediary nature. This concept was condensed and characterized in the category of software referred to in the 1980s and 1990s as 'edutainment' – software developed for the child audience that would educate while entertaining them. Although the term is no longer used to describe software because genres have been hybridized and the Internet has taken a large share of this market, the term represented the idea of intermediary space between formal learning and play, between classrooms and homes. Bridging the gap between academic and leisure-time pursuits, children's play with electronic media and their recreational use of ICTs, negotiates between the realms of home and classroom, between leisure and labour, between entertainment and education.

At the same time, the places where children now play are often 'beyond the garden wall,' outside the classroom and outside the family home. Among the most important of these new play spaces are after-school, recreational, childcare services for school-aged children. In these intermediary spaces that are neither home nor classroom, neither exclusively educational nor recreational, but somewhere in between, children are spending a lot of time at play with information technologies that disregard the distinction between tool and toy. For adults, the development of new play spaces and new playthings engenders unease because they are unfamiliar to adults while at the same time they are engaging for children and occupy their time.

Mediating media: The case of *Harry Potter and the Philosopher's Stone*

The ban against *Harry Potter* in Vacation Care provides an interesting example of the intermediary nature of OSHC services in children's lives. One school principal deemed *Harry Potter and the Philosopher's* Stone to be unacceptable for Vacation Care excursions in 2001 because the film carried a PG classification. In Australia at the time, the PG classification was given to properties that were deemed to carry 'Adult Themes' of 'supernatural or mild horror' and thus 'parental guidance' was recommended (for more information on classification across Australian media, see Chapter 4). While it is arguable that the supernatural or magical elements of *Harry Potter* are in any way 'adult,' banning the film from school-affiliated excursions was, to put it in the best light, a conservative approach. The ban deprived children of a happily anticipated holiday pleasure. In addition to the 'pure entertainment' value this film offers, seeing the film might inspire some children to read the books, or even re-read them. Given the criticism and caution waged against electronic media in children's lives, the vision of a child lazing with a book on a long summer's day might be the dream come true for many parents and educators. If the film provides an access point to the more respected element of the franchise, the literature upon which the film is based, then the ban is all the more surprising and seemingly unnecessary.

The principal's decision to ban the film from holiday programmes was based on an interpretation of the state's education guidelines for use of video in schools. The guidelines state:

> Material rated PG should not be an option for viewing at the primary school level. However, at other levels of schooling, material rated PG may be selected for viewing under the educational guidance of the teaching staff.
>
> (Department of Education, Training and Employment
> (South Australia), *Administrative and Instructional
> Guidelines*, Section Three, Part III, Division 3:
> Welfare of Students, Videotape Viewing, item 94)[1]

According to the Office of Film and Literature Classification's (OFLC) rating system at the time, the PG classification

> Signals to parents that material in this category contains depictions or references which could be confusing or upsetting, to children without adult guidance. *Material classified PG will not be harmful or disturbing to children.*
>
> Parents may choose to preview the material for their children; some may choose to watch the material with their children. Others might find it sufficient to be accessible during or after the viewing to discuss the content. (emphasis added)
>
> ('Guidelines for the Classification of Films and Videotapes
> (Amendment No. 3),' p. 7. Accessed from the
> OFLC website, www.oflc.gov.au, 8 January 2002)[2]

As these excerpts illustrate, the language used by the OFLC allowed a maximum of flexibility in determining what constitutes 'parental guidance.' While the use of the word 'parental' does suggest familial supervision, the first paragraph also uses the expression 'adult guidance.' Since OSHC staff act in *locos parentis* for children in their care, surely their attendance and participation would provide sufficient adult supervision recommended by the OFLC.

Moreover, the OFLC's guidelines (at the time) were unequivocal with respect to the impact of PG material: 'Material classified PG will not be harmful or disturbing to children.' PG films may require a little explanation for some children, but even the OFLC guidelines, at the time, indicated that *Harry Potter and the Philosopher's Stone* would not harm children. In educational circles, challenging material that stimulates discussion and explanation is often referred to as providing a 'teaching moment.' Expressions, images, sounds, and ideas that need some clarification provide an opportunity to practise the critical-thinking skills that are highly valued in education and in life through discussion, reflection, and analysis. This is true for material in any medium, but perhaps especially powerful with entertainment media, such as film, because they are so attractive, provide much pleasure, and are frequently the objects of criticism with respect to commercial culture and its place in contemporary childhood.

Although the principal's prohibition on *Harry Potter and the Philosopher's Stone* is clear, the justification for his decision is not, and most Vacation Care programmes in South Australia did go to see the film without any community objection. Applying the state's education guidelines for schools (read classrooms) to OSHC services, including Vacation Care, as this principal did, ignores several important differences between OSHC and schooling, the most fundamental of which is noted in the nomenclature, *Out* of School Hours. OSHC and classrooms are different with respect to their social purposes, their institutional structures, their use of physical space, and the contributions they make to children's lives. The education guidelines were designed for application to instructional, educational, classroom settings and not for recreational programmes that occur beyond the time and space of formal instruction, in services such as before- and after-school care and Vacation Care. Indeed the principal's decision may have been based on a range of other 'community' concerns, but his justification, as it was understood by the OSHC Service Directors attending my workshop, was explicitly and specifically linked to schooling issues and not to childcare. I am aware of only one school – a public school – that implemented and maintained a ban on *Harry Potter* for the summer holidays that year. This occurred at a public school in South Australia.[3]

Aside from *Harry Potter*, however, the presence of film and video entertainment in OSHC is a recurrent, if informal, concern for services. Parental interest is occasionally voiced on both sides of the issue: OSHC services get complaints that not enough PG material is screened and, conversely, that only G material should be available. The parents who voice an opinion, however, are in the minority, and Department of Education and Children's Services (DECS) staff have told me that parental concern for video and television use is most frequently voiced by middle-class parents. Other research has confirmed this tendency elsewhere (Gailey, 1993; Seiter, 1995, 1999). The implication in such assertions by staff is that middle-class parents do not have more serious problems to attend to and thus have time to concern themselves more intimately with their children's media practices. For OSHC services, the practical solution to what we might call the 'PG problem' is to require written permission from the child's guardian for each cinema excursion. This is the route most commonly taken by OSHC services and it remains unchallenged, despite the existence of guidelines restricting use of PG material in classrooms.

Interestingly, less attention is paid to the use of video in OSHC services. PG-classified material is often screened on video and it usually goes without remark from parents. OSHC staff do not show much concern or even awareness of copyright regulations with respect to video screenings. Though media is more readily available and accessible to children in OSHC, DECS does not have guidelines specific to media use in OSHC, as it does for classrooms.

The absence of guidelines for media use in OSHC is the result of a broader misunderstanding of the limits of technology. In regulatory discourse, media are often decontextualized. That is to say, media are treated as if their meanings are singular and consistent because it is assumed that they can be understood irrespective of their physical or social placement. The ways in which specific media are deployed by particular users (or groups of users), in particular environments are often reduced to a technological gloss. So, to DECS, television is television, no matter where it is found. If television is the same in every context, then there is no need for guidelines specific to OSHC.

In *Ambient Television* (2001), a study of television in public places, Anna McCarthy shows how considering television as 'site-specific … focuses attention on the ways in which the audiovisual and material forms of TV blend with the social conventions and power structures of its locales' (p. 2). McCarthy examines the 'flexibility and adaptability of TV technology' that becomes more clear when we consider the different ways in which television operates in different circumstances (p. 3). The same can be said of other media and for the ways in which children engage with media in different environments. Through a careful examination of children's media use in OSHC, it becomes clear that the social and physical placement of these media contour the ways in which they are used.

There is more at stake though than the site-specific nature of media play and use in OSHC. Classrooms, I would argue, are work sites – the places where children engage in labour – what goes on in classrooms is more highly regarded than the leisure activities of childcare centres. We pay more attention to the activities of classrooms and thus media use comes under scrutiny frequently enough to warrant guidelines for use. Secondly, for a long time, children's leisure was conducted outside classrooms and away from school grounds. Children's leisure time has been the responsibility of parents traditionally, not governments. Since children's leisure was, for so long, a familial responsibility, we have not regulated recreation and leisure to the same extent that we have regulated schooling. Moreover, despite a long history of media classification and consumer advice, media consumption has been a private concern, not a public one. While the government has issued advice on media content, it is the responsibility of parents and families to consider that advice and to act upon it, if they so choose. Although media have not been an important part of education, they are an important part of leisure and recreation. The fact that there are no guidelines for media use in OSHC shows that we have not kept up with the growing importance of either childcare or entertainment media to our children's leisure. One could add that the guidelines for classroom media use are also quite spare as they do not account for a wide range of media, but reflect only the most widely circulating fears about television and film. Children's access to newspapers, for instance, is not specifically mentioned in the guidelines, even though reading, rather than viewing, might be a regular activity in classrooms.

The nature of Harry Potter, as a licensed property with an extensive brand identity, shows how complicated the labour/leisure divide can be. The film and its home with Warner Bros., who own specialty shops and a US television network, conjure up what Marsha Kinder (1991) calls the 'supersystem of entertainment' that manifests in 'transmedia intertextuality.' Harry Potter-licensed consumer products are readily available in the full array, including stationery, manipulative toys, character-based toys (plush toys, dolls, and action figures), board games, clothing, and more. The 'official' Harry Potter website is maintained by Warner Bros. and includes a 'Wizard's Shop' from which merchandise can be purchased online (www.harrypotter.warnerbros.com). The school principal's ban on *Harry Potter*, temporarily, detours children's access to the rich system of narrative intertextuality, of which the film is only one part.

The detour is temporary because children would most likely have had access to other Harry Potter-licensed goods and affiliated services, such as books, websites, games, and toys while attending Vacation Care.

(The Australian schools' summer holiday is coincident with Christmas.) Even without the overt presence of the film but relative to the brand identity of Harry Potter (and many other franchises), OSHC provides an intermediary space for children's media consumption and production because the 'supersystem' is, by definition, bigger than any one of its elements and it crosses the porous boundary between home, classroom, and elsewhere. At the time, it was nearly impossible to avoid being touched by the magic of Harry Potter in a media-rich society.

On the one hand, children's media objects are shaped by their relationships with other media objects. The film was made because the books were so popular. The toy figurines and other goods are marketed on the wave of the film's success. Children's media objects, however, also acquire meaning through their use. Media use is not scripted nor inscribed in the content or technology, and meaning is better understood as a set of processes under negotiation, often shaped by environmental and contextual factors. As Jonathan Bignell (2000) makes clear in his analysis of Action Man, although such media properties are marketed with themes that suggest how to play with them, children do not have to follow these 'scripts.' Children's play is influenced by the social context in which play occurs, including who they play with. Similarly, media play in OSHC is continually under negotiation at individual, peer, institutional, and market levels. At OSHC and in play, children use media in flexible, mobile, and transformative ways that often challenge the intentions of manufacturers and marketers.

Throughout this book I examine children's media access and use in the intermediary space of OSHC. In arguing that OSHC is an intermediary space between home and school, I am defining a 'third place,' as Sony mobilized the expression in their PlayStation 2 marketing campaign.[4] Sony's Middle East-region website described a place where media platforms converge but do not necessarily merge:

Most people live in two places – the work place including school, college, or office, and the home. But, with the PlayStation 2, people can now enter what Sony calls The Third Place – a place where one can free the mind and open up to the unlimited personal entertainment experiences.

Access to The Third Place is possible because PlayStation 2 combines several state-of-the-art technologies which will enable consumers to choose the widest range of entertainment options. PlayStation 2 offers a wide selection of PlayStation 2 & PlayStation games, DVD video, DVD-ROM, Audio CD playback, and in the future, broadband internet [*sic*] access.

(http://www.sony-middleeast.com/aboutus/07FEB01.htm, accessed 11 January 2002)

In the intermediary space of OSHC, children's media use is mediated by the standards, goals, and moral imperatives of formal schooling, life in the nuclear family, and the structures that guide activities in the unique setting that is neither home nor classroom but a third place. That third place is OSHC. In Chapter 3, I explain what I mean by intermediary space and demonstrate how OSHC mediates a child's day temporally and spatially, between home and classroom. Most importantly, I discuss how the intermediary nature of OSHC provides unique access to the range of media that are found in both the home and classroom. Structures of media access and use, as well as systems of media management, in OSHC differ from those of both home and school. Perhaps of most interest to media scholars, children's media use in OSHC is quite different from that observed and reported for homes and classrooms.

Similar to findings from studies in Great Britain, Europe, and North America, two major studies of Australian children's media use have identified a need to account for children's media use *outside* the well-studied sites of home and classroom (Kaiser Family Foundation, 1999; Livingston and Bovill, 2001; Meredyth et al., 1999; OFLC, 1999). OSHC is one of the most important of these sites because it is an everyday and informal leisure-time environment and, unlike similar services in the US and UK, media play is considered an acceptable activity and it is among the most popular with children. Although the Australian school system shares many aspects of the US and UK systems, OSHC, as part of child-care services rather than educational services, is more similar to child-care provisions for school-aged children in Sweden, Norway, and Denmark. Australian childcare, along with such provisions as in Sweden, Norway, and Denmark, has been described as a case of 'maximum public responsibility,' while the US and UK exemplify the trend of 'maximum private responsibility' (Brennan, 1998: 1). This characterization is mainly related to breadth of provision and government subsidy of such services, but there are other features in common with the Nordic countries as well.

Attitudes towards children's media use for entertainment and recreation appear to be more closely aligned with views in northern Europe than they are with attitudes in the US and UK. The combination of factors, breadth of provision, government subsidy of childcare, and a welcoming attitude towards media play, makes Australian OSHC a particularly interesting location for the study of children's recreational media use, and one that will be valuable to researchers and practitioners outside Australia. A brief history of childcare in Australia is provided in Chapter 2.

Intermediary space

OSHC provides a social space that mediates between the spaces of home and classroom. As far as media play is concerned, theorizing OSHC as 'intermediary space' allows me to reassert the idea of mediation in the study of children's media use. Rather than re-runs of the 'plug-in drug' or other variations on 'hypodermic,' media effects theories made popular in the 1970s and sadly still holding currency, intermediation reminds us that media play is always mediated and never dictated. Children's media practices are not framed by film, television, or computer screen, but are, as social practices, shaped and constructed within the different spaces that children occupy and subject to the social regulations operating in those environments. As social actors, children contribute to the shape of these spaces and the cultures of these places. Between spaces and across media platforms, a child's overall media competency is thus formed through processes of negotiation that incorporate influences from both private places and public institutions, formal instruction and informal learning.

The more we know about children's actual media preferences, pleasures, and practices, the less likely we will be to subscribe to inflammatory reports of media effects or to propose technological responses to social concerns. The 'V-chip' and Internet-filtering software are supposed to help manage children's access to media content, but they operate at a technological rather than a social level.

When we bar children from experiencing particular content, we also bar them from learning and practising self-management. If they are not given the opportunity to make informed decisions for themselves, they will not be able to practise this essential skill. The more we know about children's media practices, the better equipped we will be to assist children in becoming responsibly self-monitoring, self-regulating agents, happy with their own media consumption and production. Active regulation and censorship, even if facilitated by technological solutions such as filtering software, are expensive, paternalistic, patronizing, and on occasion punitive, responses to the increased appeal that popular media hold for children. If, as many theorists have suggested, the boundaries between adulthood and childhood are ever blurring, perhaps the most important contribution that adults can make is to provide the resources that enable children to become independent and responsible media consumers and producers. Intermediary spaces, such as OSHC, are places where children are allowed to exercise a degree of independence and demonstrate self-management in play, including play about and with media and ICTs.

This approach is consistent with the position of the Carnegie Council of Adolescent Development, which, in its report, 'Great Transitions: Preparing Adolescents for a New Century (1995), has advocated for youth media training 'in community and youth development programs ... to imbue teenagers with critical habits of mind ... to help them become effective users of technology, restoring personal control'. A similar position is taken by Honorine Nocon and Michael Cole (2006: 117) when they argue that after-school programmes are valuable precisely for their 'informal and tenuously institutionalized nature.' In a guide for parents and carers of young children, the US Cable in the Classroom and National PTA (Parent Teacher Association) assure adults that media use can support child development and they recommend avoiding 'heavy-handed blanket restrictions' on children's media use in favour of strategies for media use that 'harness the best aspects of media for their children' (2004: 19). OSHC services give children the opportunity to develop their media competency and manage their own media play.

Media competency or media literacy: What's the difference?

I use the term 'media competency' to refer to a child's overall knowledge, skill, and habits of media use, instead of the more familiar and highly charged phrase, 'media literacy.' There is great debate within the field of media studies about the fundamental question: what constitutes 'literacy?' Following from this confusion is another set of debates about how curriculum should approach the task of teaching media literacy: Is media literacy defined as the ability to decode or understand media forms, or does it also demand the ability to produce media in different forms? How many levels of understanding are necessary to deem one 'media literate'? Questions such as these recur throughout the literature.

Statements on media literacy often imply that understanding of media industries and the production practices that affect texts are the key issues. Media literacy programmes often focus on understanding sponsorship practices in commercial media (television especially) and editorial point of view in journalism and news. This perspective does not account for literacy as pleasure and generic knowledge. David Buckingham explains how children use generic knowledge to help quash their uneasy feelings about fictional material:

> [C]hildren also develop forms of generic knowledge – or 'media literacy' – which enable them to cope specifically with media experiences. For example, they will attempt to predict the outcome of a narrative on the basis of their previous experience of the genre; they will use information from beyond the text, both from conversations with others and from publicity material of various kinds; and they will use their understanding of how the illusion of realism is created.
>
> (Buckingham, 2000: 135)

Since fundamental debates have not been resolved in half a century and the term media literacy only accounts for certain types of literacy, it is a troubling term and not helpful enough. If we seek to account for the ways in which children's media play contributes to their overall knowledge of media and consequent uses of media, the concept of competency is a more inclusive, and thus more useful, term.

I also prefer the term media competency to media literacy because the idea of competency does not share associations with print literacy and thus, is not obligated to similar standards or programmes of delivery when considering curriculum design. While literacy is most often associated with formal schooling, competency can be understood to include the range of practices and skills a person acquires over a lifetime and in many different circumstances. Media literacy, as Renee Hobbs (1998) has noted in the essay 'The Seven Great Debates in the Media Literacy Movement,' has emphasized 'learning and teaching of these skills through using mass media texts in primarily school-based contexts' (p. 16).[5] Unlike literacy, competency can include the objects, media, and social practices that are ignored, discouraged, or even forbidden in schooling. Competency can account for the informal learning that is significant when we are talking about an individual's full range of media practices. Media competency can include the whimsy of play and the learning that occurs during leisure, both of which are sometimes counter to the rigour and goal-oriented nature of activities deemed more serious by adults.

Additionally, one would think that media literacy describes a functional fluency with media, in all of its forms, because that is what is suggested by the combination of terms in the phrase, media and literacy. Media literacy is a phrase that more often describes a programme or curriculum in the first instance and only secondarily refers to a set of skills that the individual possesses independent of an instructional environment. While Julian Sefton-Green (2003) is correct in stating that 'there is no consensus about what informal learning might be,' and Daniel Schugurensky (2006) has characterized informal learning as 'a residual category of a residual category' because it is neither formal or non-formal education, the concept of informal learning is useful in thinking about the acquisition of media skills and competency in OSHC.

Following Livingstone (2006), informal learning, the type that occurs in OSHC, is distinguished from formal learning by the degree of agency that the learner has and the centrality of a set curriculum. In an informal learning situation, the teacher does not have more agency or authority in the learning agenda than the learner and there is no appeal to an organized body of knowledge (a curriculum) (Livingstone, 2006: 204). Learner assessment, sorting, and rationalization are not significant to informal learning (Nocon and Cole, 2006: 117). Understood in these terms, it is clear that the type of learning that occurs around media play in OSHC is informal. The activities are child-directed in the main; peer tutelage is the most prominent form of 'instruction'; there is no explicit curriculum; and there is no formal assessment or evaluation of learning (although children may form opinions of the abilities of their peers). Media literacy is, to the contrary, highly formalized and guided by a sense that without formal instruction in 'how to read/interpret' media, children will be victimized by media.

Finally, media literacy is most often discussed in reference to children and youth, and not adults. Reviewing the literature, one could not be faulted for thinking that adults are either media literate by virtue of their age or are beyond the need for such literacy. In most definitions of media literacy there is an assumption that adults know these things and children do not. 'The media' and 'the child' are often objectified and then poised as adversaries against one another with media posing a nearly indefensible threat to children. Such views of 'the media' and 'the child' have helped sustain a protectionist agenda. Often the articulated goal of media literacy is to give children tools with which they will be able to defend themselves against the dangers of media. Often the objects that are deemed most threatening are precisely those that children find most appealing. The main goal of media literacy courses is often critical consumption and not creative production, although production is sometimes mentioned as an ideal outcome but one that is difficult to achieve. Ironically, the objects that children are meant to be critical of are precisely those that they enjoy. This makes the media literacy project a difficult one. Overall, the dominant perspective associated with 'media literacy' is that media are capable of harming children while adults, somehow, are immune to these purported effects.

I find this last issue quite disturbing for its logic. If danger lurks in media, adults should be just as susceptible to it as children. Media literacy, if it is at all like linguistic literacy, is a process that begins outside of curriculum and is embedded in our everyday practices and ways of thinking in a media-rich culture. Linguistic literacy is cumulative, social, and ever expanding. Like a toddler whose vocabulary seems to grow by the hour, our competency with media is also continually enhanced and often part of a larger social exchange. The meaning of a film or television programme can depend upon the circumstances of the viewing, who one is with, the social tenor of the group, and other social factors that might influence the reception of a particular film, game, or programme.

A preschool child acquires knowledge and skill with media in a way similar to processes of language learning and use. A preschool child, often as young as 18 months, is aware of social conventions and codes in many media practices. As an example of how early we begin to learn the social codes of media, a story about an infant in a large family is illustrative. While sharing a cup of tea with me, a friend and mother of five put her three-month-old in his capsule (baby seat), on the floor, among his three sisters as the girls played a board game. When they finished their game, the girls turned around to watch TV. After a moment, they realized that their baby brother was no longer in their circle. The five-year-old said, 'Lewis can't see the TV,' and then she turned the capsule around and dragged the baby into the semi-circle. The sisters included their baby brother in a group-viewing event because television, especially in family households, is often a group activity and part of social discourse.

The first sentence I heard my eldest nephew speak, as he toddled across the lounge room in nothing but a nappy with his toddler tummy sticking out, was 'Whatcha' watchin'?' As he strolled across the room directly obscuring his father's precious view of the basketball game, he turned his head and asked this question with casual elegance. My brother (the child's father) answered, 'The ball game. Basketball.' 'Oh – ball,' my nephew replied in staccato toddler-ese. He then waddled over to the pile of toys across the room and began to sort and arrange primary-coloured plastic toys, as toddlers do. He ignored the television, ignored the company, and got down to toddler business.

Even though he was not interested in this programme, the simple question 'Whatcha' watchin'?' suggests he had rudimentary knowledge of several dimensions of the television experience: the technology, its content or programming, and audience. My nephew knew that TV is watched, that people watch it with intent, and that it offers a range of content in different programmes (the 'what' in his question). That is a lot for a child to know about TV before the age of two.

Of course a toddler (and some adults arguably) does not know the difference between fiction and non-fiction, between serial and special event, between commercial and public broadcasting, or a wide range of other industrial, aesthetic, and narrative distinctions that are fundamental to television forms. Nevertheless a toddler can possess a functional competency with respect to certain media (broadcast television, some genres of print media, radio, and music). Of course a toddler does not know that children's book publishing is a highly competitive industry, but we do not dismiss the child's growing print literacy because s/he only has a toddler-level understanding of publishing. To the contrary, all the experts advise that we read stories, poems, and letters – whatever the child will listen to and engage with – because these experiences build the communication skills essential to reading, writing, speaking, and thinking. The same should hold true for electronic, entertainment media, such as computers and television. They are part of our social surroundings, part of our culture, and their presence cannot, and should not, be viewed as wholly or necessarily detrimental.

A person's media competency is acquired across a lifetime, in a variety of circumstances, and well before entering a classroom or being exposed to formal curriculum and instruction. Media literacy programmes, on the other hand, like most school learning, are organized around certain learning objectives, and are often evaluated for achievement of quantifiable skills. As Faith Rogow, President of the Alliance for a Media Literate America (AMLA), has argued, even the idea that preschool children possess or should possess media competency will be met with resistance because so many people believe that such young children should not be involved with media. In arguing for an 'ABCs' of media literacy, Rogow (2002) points out how absurd this position really is:

> While that belief is based on genuine concern for children's well-being, it is based more on inference than actual research and it begs the pedagogical issue of how to develop literacy skills without exposing people to the materials we hope they will learn to 'read.'
> (http://www.medialit.org/reading_room/article566.html)

I am not arguing that media literacy classes or lessons are not useful. I am proposing that we expand our concept of media literacy so that we can include informal learning, in addition to the formal, curriculum-based learning. By the time a child has entered school, s/he is well along in the process of acquiring media competency. For this reason, I prefer to speak of a child's media competency because the term media literacy has acquired an association with particular teaching/learning programmes that do not, and most likely cannot, account for a person's lifelong acquisition of media competency. Similar to the way in which a child's print literacy is commonly developed before entering school and outside the classroom, our knowledge, skills, and habits of media, our growing media competency, are also developed through a range of experiences that take place in many different spaces. The notion of media competency allows us to include the informal learning that goes on at home, in play environments, through peer groups, and across a lifetime.

I am arguing that we shift the focus of attention from adult-centred, classroom-based curriculum to child-centred media practices that include recreational media among the positive experiences that children have with media. Not all media play is dangerous or harmful. While media literacy is associated with classrooms and curricula, set times for lessons and practice, media play is something that happens in many different places, in leisure time, and can be achieved to satisfaction in sessions of varying duration. Media literacy is something adults want children to acquire; media competency is something children possess and extend through play, irrespective of adult desires. Moreover, media play can be utilized to achieve particular learning outcomes that are often valued in media literacy programmes. If we want to teach children how to produce media as well as consume it, we need to know what they already do with media, what their social practices and preferences are, and what they make from it and with it.

Media competency suggests social application beyond the immediate 'lesson' and capitalizes on child-centred media practices, like those mobilized in play. Acknowledging children's everyday, recreational media practices as important to their media competency allows us to expand our view of media education to include the experiences that occur beyond the classroom. Chapter 8 describes an OSHC movie-making project as an example of informal media education.

Discovery (research methods)

In researching this book, I employed qualitative methods with a child-centred approach to discover how children's media play is situated among other media practices and how their media competency develops across the spaces they inhabit with regularity. The advantages of qualitative research methods are eloquently summarized by Berry Mayall in her essay on 'Children and Childhood' (1999):

[R]ecent sociological and anthropological approaches to children and childhood have certain distinctive features. Firstly, childhood is regarded as a constituent part of the social order, and not as a preparatory stage. Secondly, children are understood as constituting a social group, with their own specific relationships with other social groups, notably with adults and, more generally, power structures; and, complementary to those relationships, their own specific experiences and understandings of childhood. Thirdly, within interactive paradigms, children's learning and experience are understood as the site of complex political tensions between children, parents and the state ... Fourthly, children are regarded as social actors, who have purpose, and who influence as well as being influenced; as people who construct relationships and childhoods, and who can report on and discuss their experience.

(p. 12)

These characteristics provide the essential foundation upon which this qualitative work has been constructed.

My goal is a somewhat modest one: to begin the process of filling the gap in our knowledge and literature on children's media practices. I began with the assumption that like most other human activities, children's understandings, pleasures, and practices relative to media are generated not only in the space of the family home or the school's computer classroom but also in the spaces in between. I also took the view that media are more than their technological make-up; the social and physical settings in which media exist are significant to how they are experienced. In the rhythm of their everyday activities, children migrate across and between social spaces, which are often regulated by different sets of values and different standards. And yet children are able to manoeuvre with ease between the various places and their differing systems of media management. The body of knowledge that a child has about media does not respect the boundaries between classroom and home but is truly an embodied knowledge that is as mobile as the child. In order for children to negotiate the shifts in social terrain, knowledge of media and their systems of management must reside with the child and migrate with the body. Between home, classroom, after-school care, and elsewhere, children are able to manage their media use with sensitivity for the subtle differences between the regimes that structure each of these places. It is for these reasons that I examine children's media use in OSHC as a social practice and not as a social problem.

The participating OSHC services were selected with the assistance of staff from the state's Department of Education, Training and Employment (DETE), now known as DECS. We sought to include services of varying sizes, catering to different socio-economic strata. All the services selected are in the greater metropolitan area of Adelaide, the capital city of South Australia. One service was selected because media production (video making) was part of its programme.

In total, ten sites were considered for inclusion in the study. Eventually, seven were selected to participate. This is more than originally planned, but the contribution that each service could make to the study was desirable. Among the seven sites selected, only one service was eliminated during the process of securing permission from School Council. This service was undergoing a change of staffing due to illness and they were difficult to contact. Several attempts were made to include the service but circumstances proved too difficult. Finally, the study included six OSHC services.

Observations were conducted at all six sites, and interviews with children were held at five. On the basis of attendance records, approximately 250 children would have been included in the observation stage. Following the 'Interview Form' (see Appendix 2), 119 children were interviewed. Where statistics are reported across the six sites, the sample population is 119. This reflects a gender division of 65 boys and 54 girls. At the service where interviews were not conducted, the children met with me in small groups to discuss their movie-making activities. Throughout this book, quotes from children are taken from these interviews and from conversations overheard while conducting observations.

Regional and rural sites were not included in the study because conducting research in these areas was beyond the financial means of the project. South Australia is a geographically large state with vast distances in between the economic/political centre, Adelaide, and the outlying regions. Repeating a similar study in rural and regional services is recommended for further study because the financial and social circumstances in these communities are considerably different from urban and urban-fringe communities represented here. One could expect to find different configurations of media resources and media use in regional and rural services. For instance, in some areas, unique public or community media services and outlets may provide additional places for children's media use, while family homes may not provide any access at all.

Owing to the need to balance research and teaching schedules, this study focussed on the after-school care component of the participating OSHC services. Each of these services also operates before-school care and Vacation Care programmes. While contextual information about these other service components is included from time to time within this book, the focus of the research was limited to the after-school care hours. It is clear, however, that like the classroom and family home, before-school and Vacation Care programmes also influence what occurs in after-school care and they share fundamental operating principles.

The first phase of research was to observe the operation of each service and record the range and timing of activities, with special attention to media use and media play. Approximately 30 hours of observation was conducted at each site. Researchers sat near the different media areas to observe and record the children's activities and conversations during play. Researchers sometimes asked questions of the children while they played. OSHC staff were interviewed about their views of children's media use and asked to identify any problems or concerns that they had about children's media play in OSHC. During this time, consent to interview children individually was secured from parents and guardians (see Appendix 1, 'Consent Form').

After familiarizing ourselves with the daily routines of each service, the rhythms of play, and how media play fitted in with other, more traditional, forms of play, interviews with children were initiated. By this time, the children were comfortable with the presence of the research staff because we had been observing the OSHC site and its activities for two or three weeks and had become a regular presence. Researchers visited the services independently. There was never a team of researchers present but only one researcher observing and asking questions of the children. When the interview process began, most children were eager to talk with the researcher because the children had already been acting as expert informants during the observation stage. The children were also told that their comments might appear in a book. Many looked forward to being tape-recorded and they often asked if they could take a look at the laptop computer that researchers used.

The interviews were semi-structured. Each child was asked the same set of questions (see Appendix 2, 'Interview Form'), but researchers asked children to expand on their replies with prompts, such as 'tell me more about that' or 'explain why that's your favourite' and 'tell me again, what do you like about that video game?' The children's responses were narrative and not simple yes or no replies to survey questions. Given that children have individual differences in media access at home and its use in general, as well as in age and personality, their responses varied in depth and level of articulation. The semi-structured approach allowed researchers to go into greater depth by asking follow-up questions to children, who easily volunteered information and to rephrase questions for those children who were less willing, less articulate, or less interested in the process. With children who were reluctant or disinterested in the interview process, we tried to secure responses to the range of questions. We found that five- and six-year-old children were much less expressive and less engaged with the interview process, but we still tried to solicit responses from them because, as a minority of the study population, their views were important in discovering the needs of younger children. It is sometimes suggested by OSHC staff that programming for the majority of children may mean that the needs of the minority of younger children become secondary. Programming refers to the specific activities offered in services as opposed to the services themselves. For instance, cooking projects are a type of programme. With respect to programming media activities, video and game classification may be an area that deserves particular attention by staff to ensure that older and younger children are provided with engaging material that is challenging to their abilities, appropriate to their tastes, and not boring. We attempted to gain as much representation as possible from participants at the younger end of the age spectrum.

The interview outline underwent one change during research. In designing the initial form, I had overlooked to include Game Boy as a video game platform. After conducting interviews at two services, it became clear that children were identifying Game Boy as a video game platform. When asked, what type of video game they had at home, many children responded, 'Game Boy.' On the first form, we wrote this response in by hand but then revised the form to include it among the choices that we identified for them in a 'yes/no' survey of their home media.

Interviews took between 15 minutes and half an hour each, depending upon how much the child had to say. Interviews were conducted individually because speaking with children in pairs made audio recording difficult, and children were often more interested in their peers than in the questions we were asking. After trying a few paired interviews we abandoned that method and spoke with children one-to-one, generally in an adjacent alcove or quiet space to secure a good sound recording. While speaking with the children we made notes on the interview form, either on the laptop or on paper. These notes were helpful when transcribing the audio tapes.

During the interview phase, observations continued with greater attention to the detail of media play. Having gained an understanding of the general operations of the service, we were able to focus on individual media and individual children. We came to know the habits of individual children and play groups. In some cases, we were able to address our observations in the interviews by asking additional questions specific to something we had seen. In this way, the observations informed the interview process even after the interview template had been designed. If this method has reduced the consistency between the interviews conducted from one service to the next, a trade-off benefit has been gained in localizing the interview questions to suit the activities unique to each service. This strategy is consistent with the view that each place, be that an OSHC service, home, or classroom, manages media use in a way that reflects local community values.

The interviews also gave us cause to revisit the observation. As we learned through the interview process what children valued and what occupied their interests, we began to look for these activities, if we had not already noticed them in our initial observations. The interviews and observations were integrated in this fashion throughout the research, continually informing one another.

2
Childhood and Childcare in Australia

> Capitalist expansion and new technologies at the end
> of the twentieth century are fundamentally altering
> the private/public divide on which the institutions of
> family and childhood rest
> —Jyotsna Kapur, 1999: 134

Unpacking Kapur's provocative remark requires that we ask how such fundamental changes are being accommodated at individual and institutional levels. If the institutions of family and childhood are unstable, what institutions or other resources are positioned to replace them? Where would we begin to replace or rework our understandings of childhood and family, or has this process already begun? What is the role of childcare in the present (re)configuration of the public/private divide? How does childcare for school-aged children in particular fit into this set of relations? And what roles do media and technologies serve? To answer these questions, we must examine the position of childcare within the broader context of childhood as a set of ideas and ideals.

The institutions of family and childhood have never been stable or monolithic; they have always been interdependent on other institutions and systems that structure the social dimensions of everyday life. Adult employment and work patterns are but two of the systems that affect families and childhood. In the twenty-first century, adults often work further from home or for longer hours than they have done under other economic systems or in other periods of history. More families now rely on two incomes and therefore, to accommodate adult schedules, children are looked after in a variety of care arrangements that often do not rely upon the services of family relations. Professional (public and private) childcare services are one of the mechanisms with

29

which adults manage a balance between the responsibilities of domestic life and public life.

Of particular interest to this work is a related question that arose in the early stages of research: why is it that attitudes towards media play in Out of School Hours Care (OSHC) in South Australia seem so generous and welcoming when compared to American (US) and British attitudes? When I worked in after-school care in California, several years ago, the only media around were the cast-off 'educational software' titles such as *Where in the World is Carmen Sandiego* and *The Oregon Trail*. These are terrific games, for sure, but they do not create a media landscape like that found in Australian OSHC services. In my subsequent research trips to the US in the last eight years, I have not seen significant change in media provision, and the literature confirms my observations. For the US and UK, it is difficult to find more than an aside on media, with the exception of computers receiving the odd mention. On the rare occasion when there is a remark from a US perspective on television, video, or video games, it is usually critical. Media use in childcare is characterized disparagingly as a form of 'electronic babysitter' and media play is less respected than other forms of play. It often falls prey to that facile characterization of media as 'passive' entertainment and thus, not worthwhile.

Scholarly research in Australia has been equally neglectful of media's place in childcare, but unlike the US and UK, in Australia electronic entertainment are plentiful in OSHC and objections to their presence are rare. I suggest that the relatively uncritical attitudes about media play in OSHC are best understood in the context of other ideologies, most importantly childhood, mothering, and childcare.[1] OSHC provides an interesting case study in which we can see how these ideologies influence our views of media and what we deem appropriate leisure activity for children.

OSHC in Australia has taken on its unique shape owing to a number of factors both material and ideological. In the material sense OSHC was purposefully developed to assist *women* to take advantage of opportunity within the workforce. When the services were first instituted, mainly women had responsibility for their children's care outside school hours. Now the official line is that OSHC assists families because, at least rhetorically if not in practice, children are not the sole responsibility of women. In ideological terms, OSHC bears the hallmark of dominant Australian views on family, mothering, childhood, and childcare. These views influence attitudes towards media play in OSHC and the inclusion or exclusion of both entertainment and information technologies within childcare services.

Although Australian families are increasingly reliant upon childcare services provided outside the home by professional care workers instead of family members, nineteenth-century ideals of middle-class family life, where one parent remains outside the workforce, still influence our views of childcare and our provision of childcare services and programmes. Placing a child in OSHC is often considered to be a poor substitute for spending time with a parent or relative in the family home. Parents, and mothers especially, whose work schedules do not permit them to be home when school is finished, may feel as if they are not adequately serving their children's needs when children are made to attend childcare in addition to school. Parents may feel that they bear a social stigma for utilizing childcare services, especially OSHC, because it is seen as time that the child spends away from home *in addition* to the time already given to schooling. Underlying such views is the belief that school is to children what work is to adults and that home is the ideal location for children's leisure and recreation. It is precisely because these are the dominant views of childcare that OSHC in South Australia maintains such a high-quality standard. A fundamental principle of OSHC is that it will provide for children an experience equivalent to what they would have if they were at home. Underlying this position is a view that children belong at home because homes are necessarily good places to be. In short, home is the ideal place for leisure and recreation. Relatedly, media entertainment belongs to the domain of leisure and that is increasingly for children experienced outside the home, in childcare settings.

Women at home and caring for children

As late as the 1940s in Australia, journalists and writers of popular advice to women maintained that women were necessary to the effective and glorious running of a household. Historian B. W. Higman argues that until the 1960s, in Australia, women's place in life was in the home. Higman summarizes the dominant view with a quote from a Brisbane journalist writing in the 1940s: '[T]he home is the base of our civilisation. It is there that children are trained to become good citizens.' And in a book on middle-class homes, Higman says the author 'argued against socialist childcare systems which did not fit the Australian national characteristic as home lovers' because the author believed 'good homes will be the foundation of an ideal British state' (2002: 4). To this day, while Australia is a highly urbanized nation, most of its population living in cities and suburbs, high-density housing is rare because home ownership has been affordable. According to historian

Kerreen Reiger, the ideology of family life has been reinforced in Australia by the 'ideology and actual patterns of home ownership' (1985: 38). Australians continue to enjoy an extremely high rate of home ownership and most live in suburban environments, despite the endurance of an outback/frontier mythology that is most notable in images of the nation that Australia exports abroad.

Women's relatively late arrival to the workforce helped sustain the national ideology of homemaking. As late as 1966 married women were legally prohibited from working for the Commonwealth Public Service, and strong labour lobbies ensured that men's wages remained high. The concept of a 'family wage' has been significant since the Harvester Judgment of 1907. This law guaranteed a minimum wage for every working *man* based on the assumption that men had to provide for a wife and children. While the family wage was certainly a victory for the labour force, it effectively excluded married women from that same workforce. The situation was tautological. The family wage assisted women to remain outside the workforce to care for their children at home, while a lack of childcare services and a tradition of female responsibility for children meant that women had little choice but to stay at home and care for their children.

In the efforts to populate Australia, childbearing and mothering have been important duties with nationalist undertones at various times. High regard for motherhood goes back to the earliest penal colonies where marriage was viewed as a civilizing element of convict reform. Child rearing within these marriages, however, presented a contradiction. 'On the one hand, understandings of maternity stipulated that it was in the interests of the state for women to embrace their mothering and yet, on the other, motherhood amongst convict women was devalued and their identity as mothers was disavowed' (Damousi, 1997: 120).

In her political history of childcare in Australia, Deborah Brennan (1998) says that the brief post-war investment in childcare was not aimed at assisting women to re-enter the workforce after childbearing. Instead, it was intended to help women to have *more* children in the face of a declining birth rate, a national concern for a still young nation. Low birth rate is still a political issue in Australia. Successive governments have created and maintained incentives for childbearing. Currently this approach is even more contentious than in the past because Australia has been restrictive in its immigration policies. On the one hand, the government encourages population growth but, on the other hand, it is extremely selective in granting entry to the several thousands of people who have come to Australia at great personal risk and cost. At present, families receive a 'baby bonus' of $4000 upon the birth of a child.

This is an increase since 2003, when the bonus was $2000. Families also receive an annual tax benefit for each child.

At home with their children, mothers were expected to look after them with pleasure. In *The Disenchantment of the Home: Modernizing the Australian Family 1880–1940*, Reiger (1985) outlines how Australian households were reorganized throughout the early part of the twentieth century. She makes clear that this was not an exclusively top-down process imposed by the ruling class on the rest. Instead, she says,

> several strategies were coming from various class fractions: from an upper class with its own concerns, and from professional groups. The interests of public health reformers, town planners and architects were united with those of housing reformers and the new advocates of domestic economy. These in turn often shared a frame of reference with eugenists [sic] and reformers of infant care and childbearing. The chief common frame of reference was that of technical rationality as the dominant type of social action in modern Western society.
>
> (p. 55)

As an example of how ideologies of home, house and mothering have been traditionally intertwined, a lecture given in 1937 by the Principal of the Kindergarten Training College of Victoria is illustrative. The lecturer spoke about child's play in the backyard: 'If he [sic] plays with children in his own garden, the mother can keep a wise, unobtrusive, kindly supervision and see that difficulties do not arise' (Reiger, p. 172). Reiger sees such maternal supervision of play as an additional responsibility on women, one that they did not carry before the rise of professionals and their advice. 'Women in particular,' she says, 'were bombarded with a deliberate programmed redefinition of their role as mothers' (Reiger, p. 9).

By the end of WWII, the technicians and professionals had won the battle for management of the Australian household, including childcare practices. Deborah Brennan and Carol O'Donnell (1986) argue that women's responsibility for child rearing reached a critical status in the 1950s when theories of 'maternal deprivation' were popularized and appropriated through misinterpretation for ideological purposes (to keep women out of work). Brennan and O'Donnell write that 'maternal deprivation' theory was so pervasive that

> The New South Wales Child Welfare Department, for example, cited Bowlby's work as justification for closing such centres and argued that children cared for apart from their mothers were an impediment

to the department's goal of building a 'mentally healthy, virile and law-abiding community.'

(1986: 21)

The so-called maternal deprivation theory was derived from the work of psychiatrist John Bowlby. The thesis is more accurately described as attachment theory, and it is often referred to as 'bonding.' Bowlby argued that the overall environment of a child's early years was important and that a child needed to form attachments within that environment, in order to develop appropriately. Unfortunately, the work became known by the misleading, and overly simplified, shorthand of 'maternal deprivation' which does not accurately reflect the holistic understanding of 'environment' that Bowlby intended. More importantly, Bowlby did not study children whose mothers had jobs. Among the influential experiences that culminated in attachment theory was a study he conducted for the World Health Organization. Here Bowlby examined orphans who had lost their parents during WWII and lived in large public care facilities as a result. Indeed these children were suffering, but this was due to war and not due to work. The report was published in 1951 under the title *Maternal Care and Maternal Health*. The separation and deprivation effects that war orphans would have experienced is far more acute and enduring than the consequences a child would experience if his/her mother went off to work each day and returned in time to share an evening meal.

Although Bowlby gave a series of academic papers throughout the 1950s in Britain, an early documentary film about his work may have had greater influence in the lay community worldwide. In 1952, with research assistant James Robertson, Bowlby made the film, *A Two-Year-Old Goes to Hospital*. In real time, the film documented the process of separation that a two-year-old underwent when entering the hospital without her parents. The film's wide circulation helped popularize the theory. Although I am unable to locate details of the film's release and screening in Australia, I am certain it was known. Brennan and O'Donnell say that, within Australian teacher training colleges, the theory of 'maternal deprivation' was 'virtually gospel' during the 1950s (p. 21).

This timing coincides with the beginning of the 'full employment' years in Australia, and having children was viewed as a contribution to the growth of the nation. Mothering attained a high status, but one that would circumscribe any other activities which women undertook. Unions guaranteed wages that would support a man, his wife, and three children – the ideal family at the time – and mothers were expected to stay home and look after their children. Irrespective of her training, desire, or interest in working outside the home, a woman was not supposed to work if her husband was employed. Within this context, there was no need for wide-ranging childcare services.

In 1947, only 8.6 per cent of married women worked outside the home. The low rate of employment is understandable considering that the official wage for women was set in 1950 and it established the 'female basic wage' at 75 per cent of the male wage. In the period from 1969 to 1972 a series of reforms made the concept of 'equal pay for work of equal value' a reality and helped end the broad and institutionalized male privilege to earning. In 1961 nearly 20 per cent of married Australian women were employed outside the home and by 1971 the figure had risen to one-third. Despite the steady increase in women's employment throughout the 1960s, provision of childcare was not explicitly linked to workforce issues until the early 1970s (Brennan, 1998: 59).

Women in Australia still earn considerably less than men do, but this difference is not due to legalized wage differentials. It is more likely due to women's career choices, training paths, and a cultural tradition of providing most of the domestic services and support for family, as well as an enduring regard for motherhood, and the indeterminate practices of the 'old boy network' wherein men are more likely to groom their male colleagues for promotion rather than their female colleagues.

OSHC: Law and legacy

The present configuration of high-quality childcare in Australia developed as a result of feminist political action in the late 1960s and early 1970s. In 1972 the federal parliament passed the Child Care Act, which gave the Commonwealth a role in childcare services. Childcare was, for the first time, conceived as a national political issue and as a material necessity for women to enter and remain in the workforce. Linked to national workforce concerns, childcare outside the home began to shed its stigma.

The history of childcare in Australia prior to the 1970s did not offer many good reasons to trust in or to respect childcare. The earliest childcare practices were mainly provided to women and families who were deemed to be, for one reason or another, unfit for parenting. It is in light of this earlier history that the present Australian system was conceived and continues to distinguish itself internationally with high-quality services and affordable access.

If we were to construct a timeline of key movements in Australian childcare, the current phase would be fourth in a series. Like many institutions in Australia, the roots of childcare extend back to the original penal colonies, and, although South Australia (where research for this book was conducted) was never a penal colony, the national history of childcare which informs Commonwealth policy is relevant here. Childcare outside the family was first experienced in Australia by the children of convict women. Mothers and pregnant women who were transported or incarcerated in the colonies were allowed to take their children with them but the children were looked after in an on-site nursery until they were three. At the age of three, children were sent off to 'orphan schools' while the mother endured the remainder of her sentence (Damousi, 1997).

The second phase in the history of childcare is marked by a brief period of 'child rescue' practices which began in the late nineteenth century, when poor and neglected children were removed from their family and home or given by their parents into public care (Scott and Swain, 2002). The Kindergarten movement emerges around the same time in New South Wales and Victoria (1890–1900), with the Kindergarten Union of New South Wales established in 1895 and the Sydney Kindergarten Teacher's College opening in 1900. South Australia followed closely with the Union emerging in 1905, and in Tasmania, Queensland and Western Australia similar organizations and services emerged by the end of the decade.[2]

It is important to note that Kindergarten was neither conceived nor viewed by its advocates as a childcare service. Leaders of the Kindergarten movement in Australia were adamant that kindergarten was the first step towards formal schooling, and not a substitute for parental care. Kindergartens were first established in poor communities, but by women from the upper classes who sought to assist the poor in surviving their own circumstances. They were philanthropic organizations, privately funded and operated. Kindergartens would 'institutionalize' middle-class values for the poor.

During WWII, however, Kindergartens began to lose their class affiliation and became more widespread. In 1942 *Kindergarten of the Air* was first broadcast over radio and locally focussed Kindergartens were established by groups of women on behalf of their own families. These initiatives are the first signs of the transformation from a philanthropic endeavour to a more generic element of the education system. Between 1950 and 1959 Kindergartens sprang up across Australia, and preschool teaching gained more professional status and respect, as evidenced by scholarships for training and more government investment in preschool.

Today, working women of all classes struggle with the decision to enrol their children in Kindergarten. Not to be confused with the

US kindergarten, in Australia, 'Kindie,' as it is colloquially known, is pre-school for children from the age of four. The first year of schooling is known as Reception in South Australia and it offers a full day of school, generally six hours in total including a minimum of five and one-quarter hours of instruction, recess, and lunch breaks. Most schools begin at 9.00 a.m. Although the Kindergarten programmes are subsidized, and often reduce childcare costs overall, the timing of Kindergarten sessions is inconvenient for many working parents. Sessions operate as half-day programmes and they do not provide childcare on site after the session concludes. Many parents find the half-day sessions inconvenient because they have to pick the child up mid-way through the day, and this is challenging if there is not an adult with flexible time to go and retrieve the child. For many parents it is more convenient to skip Kindergarten entirely and continue with the less educationally oriented childcare until the child enters school. Many parents also believe that childcare now provides the same preschool preparation that in previous eras was exclusive to Kindergartens.

The third point on our timeline is the temporary expansion of child-care services during WWII. To assist women who worked outside the home in the war industries, established Kindergarten facilities operated longer hours and provided childcare, as a service distinct from their nor-mal Kindergarten sessions. The government of the time did not want to set a precedent for childcare provision after the duration and made tem-porary, rather than long-term, investments during this period.

The practice known as 'baby farming,' giving infants over to people who would claim to care for them, was not as widespread or as contro-versial in Australia as it was in the UK, according to Scott and Swain (2002). The practice is not considered a significant part of the history of childcare in Australia.

The timeline I have sketched, however, only applies to Australians of European descent. Cutting across the timeline from the late nineteenth century up until the 1960s, young Aboriginal women and girls were routinely taken from their families and put into domestic service, mainly to provide childcare to elite white families. While it was only a tiny minority of the white population who participated in this system, the practice affected Aboriginal communities extensively. The result was disastrous for Aboriginal families. Retrospectively viewed from the pres-ent, the practice bears the mark of racist policies that were perpetrated against the indigenous people of Australia and institutionalized by early administrations and consecutive governments of federal, territorial, and state jurisdictions.

While these earlier childcare practices would not have been foremost on the minds of advocates, activists, policymakers and childcare providers in the 1970s, they do provide the developmental context for current practices. They also inform how we think about and, to some degree, measure our current practices as part of social progress. They also provide points of distinction from which the ideal middle-class childhood is differentiated. In OSHC, the middle-class ideal manifests in a wide range of details, including media provision, access, and use by children.

This middle-class ideal is not without its critics. Tania Sweeney (1989) has characterized childcare in Australia as a form of 'middle-class welfare' because, since WWII, it is middle-class families who have benefited the most from government policies on childcare because these policies have prioritized childcare places for children whose parents are in the workforce.[3] While I agree with Sweeney that childcare does benefit middle-class families in Australia and I would also say that indeed the ideal of childhood is based on such middle-class aspirations for family life, I do not find her characterization of childcare as 'middle-class welfare' a particularly helpful one. It suggests that an increase in services would only further benefit the middle class and not necessarily assist families outside this socio-economic strata. It forecloses discussion of expansion of services or even improvement of services to the detriment of those currently utilizing such services and those who are not but would like to, particularly the lower socio-economic strata and the chronically unemployed.

OSHC services are conceived with reference to and measured against an image of the ideal middle-class family home. OSHC staff workers and some employees of South Australia's DECS proudly claim that OSHC aims to provide a setting and activities that are equal to that which is available to children who go home after school. Characterizing OSHC in this way indicates that the dominant social ideology maintains that going home directly from school is the preferred arrangement, the option that best meets the ideals of childhood. The imagined home is, of course, a caring, sharing, clean, safe, well-provisioned place where children willingly and happily pass their leisure time in the care of equally willing and happy adults.

This view is so pervasive that, when I raised the question of whether or not they had considered that video games and television be eliminated from OSHC, staff responded by arguing that children who go home directly from school often play video games or watch television. In the opinion of these professional childcare workers and managers, OSHC should not deprive children of the opportunity to enjoy the same entertainment and leisure-time pursuits that are available to children who are cared for in their own homes. Unwittingly, ideals (perhaps middle class) about families and homes set the standard for OSHC.

Underlying this position is a view that OSHC policy must ensure that children in public care are not disadvantaged relative to other children. A most striking exhibition of this view is voiced in an informational and training video produced by the Network of Community Activities in New South Wales. *Holiday Fun: Vacation Care for Children* (1996) opens with the following framing remark, delivered in direct address, by a Vacation Care Coordinator:

> At school holidays, a lot of people go away and have the family holiday when school holidays are on. You've got to provide the children with a good alternative to that so they don't feel like they're missing out on something by not having three weeks on the south coast catching fish or whatever. It's gotta be fun for them.

The same attitude is applied to after-school-hours care.

Fees and charges are addressed at length later but a snapshot view here is helpful. At the time of publication the average cost of after-school care in South Australia is $3.00 per hour. Most services, however, charge by the session, and an afternoon's care is approximately $9.75 for three and one-quarter hours. If a child attends five sessions per week, the average cost is less than $50 per week.

The US model for after-school care

Contrast the Australian views of after-school care with the attitudes that are expressed about similar programmes in the US and their respective funding structures. Childcare for school-aged children in the US is federally funded only in communities where children are deemed to be 'at risk,' and the programmes themselves are described in terms that derive from compensatory education and enrichment models. The schools that do not serve disadvantaged populations do not get a share of federal funding to operate their programmes; they operate as locally managed, private services on public property.

The California Department of Education describes the federal 'No Child Left Behind Act of 2001,' the most extensive source of government support for after-school care in the US, as providing grants to establish or expand

> after school programs that provide students, particularly students who attend schools in need of improvement, with academic enrichment

opportunities and supportive additional services necessary to help the students meet state and local standards in the core content areas.

(California Department of Education)

This federal funding initiative is designed to assist 'academic achievement' by reinforcing and complementing academic programmes and by contributing to 'family literacy and related educational development services.'

Similarly, California's successful 2002 Ballot Proposition 49, which sought universal after-school care, maintains the US national concern for extending the school day and compensating for deficiencies in schooling and in a family's ability to contribute to their children's education. Priority for establishing the after-school programmes is first to schools that already operate such programmes and to those which serve 'a majority of low-income students' (Voter Guide, 2002).[4] The lead spokesperson at the time for Proposition 49 was Arnold Schwartzenegger, bodybuilder, film celebrity, and soon-to-be Governor of California. Following the success of the California initiative, Schwartzenegger gave testimony to the US Senate Committee on Appropriations in May 2003, requesting that the US Congress continue its funding of the 21st Century Learning Grant Program. In his statement, Schwartzenegger argued,

If our children are our future, our future is in jeopardy every afternoon between 3:00 PM and 6:00 PM when unsupervised children roam the streets ... Every public school that chooses should have the resources to offer their unsupervised students, a safe, educationally enriching place to go after school.

(*Hearings and Testimony*, May 13, 2003,
Labor HHS Subcommittee Hearing, p. 2)

This, he said, was his aim the previous year when he sponsored the California State initiative, Proposition 49. In outlining the programmes that a 'comprehensive' after-school care service should provide, the priorities were clear: 'academics, homework assistance, reading, computer classes, and language skills' (p. 4). To his credit, Schwartzenegger further qualified his remarks by stating that a quality programme must also include 'drama, music, physical fitness, and other activities that build self-esteem, maturity, and social responsibility.'

No matter how well intentioned these efforts, they are readily distinguished from the Australian view of OSHC for their emphasis on education and crime prevention rather than children's recreation and leisure or parental and workforce need.[5] In June of 1998, at least four years prior to the initiatives outlined above, in an article on the after-school programme 'Safe and Smart,' a quality programme was described as including the following components:

> tutoring and supplementing instruction in basic skills, such as reading, math, and science; drug and violence prevention curricula and counseling; youth leadership activities; volunteer and community service opportunities; college awareness and preparation; homework assistance centers; courses and enrichment in the arts and culture; computer instruction; language instruction, including English as a second language; employment preparation or training; mentoring; activities linked to law enforcement; and supervised recreation and athletic programs and events.
>
> ('What Works,' 1998)

In this descriptive list of activities, there is no mention of play or of media. It would appear these two activities are illegitimate. The idea of after-school care in the US is entirely bound up with academic achievement, uplifting the educationally challenged or deprived, and enrichment for the advanced student. There seems to be little notion of children's need for recreation and leisure.

In a lecture to Australian Children's Services staff in 2002, Terry Petersen, former senior staff member of the US Department of Education explained that parental priorities for after-school care in the US are (1) technology learning, (2) art and music, (3) languages, (4) clubs, (5) fitness, and (6) community service (Petersen, 25 July 2002). Recreation, leisure, and play are still not among the priorities. There is clearly an orientation to learning useful skills and many of the stated priorities reflect curriculum areas that have been slowly eliminated from formal schooling in the US over the last 30 years.

Beth Miller, formerly Director of the US National Institute on Out-of-School Time (NIOST), in her opening address to conference participants at School's Out Washington (state) argued that US after-school programmes ought to be emphasizing enrichment rather than extending the school day's curriculum. Enrichment, for Miller, means offering the things that the school day does not offer so that the activities are different and children engage with them differently. She says it is not the amount of time that children spend on lessons but their engagement with them that determines whether or not they learn. She characterizes out-of-school-hours programmes as providing a border zone between home and classroom, similar to the notion of intermediary space that I have outlined, and will explain more thoroughly in the next chapter.

Miller's remarks, and those of many participants at the 2003 conference, were framed by recent funding shifts in the 21st Century Community Learning Centers. The 21st Century programmes were federally funded and administered programmes that were to provide educational opportunities for children, but 'educational' was interpreted very broadly. Since its inception in 1996, the programme has shifted emphasis to the middle-school years (Grades Six, Seven, and Eight) and focussed on safety after school hours. Jill Schmitt argues that each year the focus has moved closer and closer to an educational imperative. 'Adequate yearly progress,' or standard achievement in school, and school attendance rates are being used to measure the success of after-school programmes. How school attendance correlates with enrichment is difficult to see. It seems the success of the after-school programme is measured by attendance rates at school rather than attendance rates at after-school programmes. This clearly demonstrates how after-school care is subsumed by educational imperatives in the US rather than the workforce needs of adults or the recreational needs of children. Again, because the focus in the US is on children from lower-income families and those living in poor communities, it appears as though poor children today, like their counterparts in previous eras, still have less leisure time than children from more well-to-do families, even if they aren't engaged in waged labour.

It is difficult, at best, to compare the US provision of after-school care with that in Australia because programmes in the US are federally funded only in communities where a large percentage of the children live in low-income households or where they are deemed to be at risk. Nevertheless the type of programmes that experts in the US recommend for after-school services are similar to those offered in Australia. The difference is that in Australia, these programmes are provided as childcare services without reference to the socio-economic status of the children or their potential to be victims or perpetrators of crime or to their achievement in school. Perhaps the most important point we can take from the comparison is to recognize that what Australia currently offers to children and families is highly beneficial even if outcomes are not measurable in academic terms.

The US provision of childcare for school-aged children also differs from the Australian provision in that the American model encompasses children up to the age of 18, or when they would complete year 12 of high school. In Australia, children are defined by the ages from birth to 12 years. The Australian system does not lump youth with children but distinguishes the very different needs of these age groups. Recreation and leisure are the priorities for children in OSHC and the service to adults is defined by greater opportunity for parents to remain in the workforce. Issues of education and crime prevention are not interwoven in the Australian discourse on OSHC, with the occasional exception of statements that promote OSHC as a 'safe place' for children to play. OSHC services sometimes provide homework assistance for children but this is not universal and is based on parent request. Many Australian parents want to or are encouraged by the schools to supervise their children's homework or participate with their children in completing homework. This type of parent–child collaboration is believed to engender an investment by the parent in the child's schooling. Parental involvement with homework is also seen to enhance communication between homes and classrooms. For all of these reasons, homework is not a universal priority at OSHC and it is an exception rather than a rule.

Although I have argued that the Australian model of after-school care is based on an ideal of the family home, such home life may not even exist; many have argued that such an ideal was ever a reality only for a privileged few, if it existed in the first place. The historic reality of childhood and family life is that both have been experienced in a variety of ways relative to a range of circumstances, and most significant among these circumstances is financial. OSHC, however, seeks to provide an environment and a range of activities acceptable in present-day middle-class homes. Working against a history of childcare as a form of welfare for the under-classes, and working towards an accommodation of contemporary adult employment patterns, OSHC is a key mechanism with which families are managing changes in the public/private divide. One of those changes in Australia is the desire to realize the myth of a middle-class society, or at least a society in which the differences between rich and poor are less acute than in Australia's past and elsewhere in the present. While it is reasonable to challenge the classic mythology of middle-class life in Australia and to criticize its ideals, which include home ownership and the option for one parent to remain outside the workforce while children are in school, we must acknowledge that increasingly the middle-class family is one in which the sole parent or both parents are employed and OSHC provides a critical service to such families.

Children and childhoods: Past and present

In his seminal history, *Centuries of Childhood: A Social History of Family Life*, Philippe Aries (1962) argues that childhood and class distinction developed alongside one another with increasing description and proscription of 'child' and 'adult' from the fifteenth century to the present. At this same time, the family's relation to society was also changing and developing into what became the (insulated) nuclear family, which reached near-sacred status in the late nineteenth century. While families took on responsibility for the moral training and physical well-being of children, schools took on the task of educating them. As the role of families changed so did the role of schooling.[6]

Today the process is operating in reverse. Public institutions are being asked to take back some of the care for children that they held before the epoch of the nuclear family. Prior to confirming the nuclear family and schools as the institutions of primary care for children, a majority of children spent their days working. In the British census of 1851 (around the time that the Australian colonies were established as self-ruling entities) five million children were accounted for in England and Wales. Two million were reported as enrolled in school, 600,000 working, and the balance, nearly two and a half million children, were unaccounted for. Sally Mitchell (1996) argues that the unaccounted-for half were in fact working, but not in recognized, paid employment, so their actual status was missed by the census.

> Even in 1900, most young people were in full-time employment by the age of thirteen or fourteen. And many younger children throughout the period did the kind of work that was less visible than factory labor. The worst conditions were probably in home industries. Tedious hand-work of all sorts (e.g., box making, toymaking, painting Christmas cards, coloring fashion plates, assembling artificial flowers, putting matches in boxes, sewing buttons on cards, doing embroidery, knitting, lacemaking) was done at home by women and paid for by the piece. Mothers who did this work generally made their children help – both to keep them occupied and because their assistance was useful. If there was no other source of income, a woman and her children might have to keep steadily at work for fourteen or sixteen hours a day in order to survive. Children were trained for some of these crafts at dame schools, which also served as 'childminding' institutions while mothers earned a living. Girls and boys as young as age three or four would be put to work braiding straw (for hatmaking) or making baskets and given some instruction in reading. The work they produced paid for their schooling.
>
> (p. 45)

It is somewhat ironic that the jobs Mitchell describes as being common child labour in the mid-nineteenth century are strikingly similar to what we now call 'arts and crafts' and commonly find in many child-care services today. What was once work is now a mainstay of children's leisure. Children no longer have to toil away at 'box making, toymaking, painting Christmas cards, coloring fashion plates, assembling artificial flowers ...'; these activities are viewed as arts and crafts or, 'making' in the jargon of OSHC, and children pursue them at their leisure, for pleasure. A fundamental difference between today's children and the working children of Victorian England is that contemporary children are allowed to produce objects only for their sentimental (use) value and not for their market (exchange) value.

A sticky point in this construction is, however, children's education. Educational endeavours are understood to be of value for their future use. This is where some media activities and media play are deemed useless, for the present and the future. While the activities that used to constitute work for children are now deemed valuable leisure activities (making crafts), the newer activities of leisure, such as video game play, are often considered to be a waste of time, unless it can be shown that they complement education or lead to a future use (one that is preferably not for recreation).

While Mitchell's description of children's work accounts for the children of the labouring classes, Aries is clear to point out that the modern notion of childhood (beginning around the seventeenth century), in which the child is protected by the nuclear family, did not initially touch children from the lower classes. Their life remained for some 200 more years intimately linked with public life and work life, as Mitchell describes. Not until the reforms of the industrial revolution, which limited child labour, did poor children gain access to the idealized childhood that Aries and others have described (Merlock Jackson, 1986; Zelizer, 1985). Mitchell confirms this view and locates the emergence of the 'ideal family' more specifically: '[T]he model of mother at home, father at work, and family as the center of children's lives – the model taken as 'natural' for much of the twentieth century – had its origin in middle-class patterns of life' during the Victorian era (1996: 41). She writes:

> Despite our sentimental belief that Victorians worshipped mother-hood and family values, most mothers did not do much child care. In the working class, children looked after themselves and younger children; a seven-year-old might have almost full responsibility for the baby ... Even after schooling became compulsory, girls were kept home to look after babies. They did more work as children than boys; school records from the 1870s show girls from age nine to twelve

spending between twenty and thirty hours a week on housework, errands, and child-minding.

(pp. 146–8)

The 'benefits' of a middle-class childhood could not extend to children who worked, so it was not until labour reforms removed children from most employment that the middle-class childhood became '*the* ideal childhood.' In the 1890s, the lives of working class children came under more rigorous scrutiny, discipline, and regulation, as children rather than as workers (Mitchell: 149).

Children, consumerism, and popular culture

Viviana Zelizer (1985) argues that between 1870 and 1930 two qualities of the modern child were essentialized: their economic worthlessness and sentimental value. In the US 'by the 1930s, lower class children joined their middle-class counterparts in a new nonproductive world of childhood, a world in which the sanctity and emotional value of a child made child labor taboo' (p. 6). The debates that ensued over child labour demonstrate that the struggle involved shifting ideologies about children. Children were reconceived. While they were once significant contributors to family income, they became economically worthless, consumers rather than contributors.

> Sentimentalized views coexisted with the instrumental valuation of children in the nineteenth century, while the economic value of children persisted long after it was declared illegal and morally offensive. To this day, the economic worth of a child is still a concern, particularly in rural areas and sometimes among the urban lower class.
>
> (p. 214)

The removal of children from the workforce also coincided with a rise in urbanization. More families lived in high-density housing in the cities and their worthless children, no longer occupied in factory jobs, had free time to play. For urban children, the most accessible play space was the street. Zelizer links a rise in child death caused by vehicular accident to the movement for dedicated playgrounds, which became a priority for urban planners in the US during the early part of the twentieth century. At the same time, cities also increased prohibition on children's street-play. Parents were advised to create indoor play spaces for children, perhaps converting an unused room into a safe play area (pp. 32–55). Today there is another tidal shift and indoor play is now often demonized for its association with media and outdoor play is encouraged for its physical activity.

Media and childhood

The transformations that are occurring today, like the reforms that Mitchell, Zelizer, and others describe for previous eras, are not experienced by all children in the same way. Family socio-economic status still effects the way in which childhood is experienced although services like OSHC aim to ameliorate difference. The insulated and isolated privacy of the family no longer provides all that a child needs, and the very objects and practices that helped define the ideal childhood and its culture may now pose new threats to that ideal.

Often an objection to children's popular culture and its associated media is really an objection to mass culture as it is facilitated by mass production and distribution. Do parents object to their children really liking something a lot or is it that parents object when children like things that are so readily available that they are not equally as precious as the children themselves? In the introduction to *A Necessary Fantasy? The Heroic Figure in Children's Popular Culture* (2000), a collection on children's popular culture, editors Dudley Jones and Tony Watkins explain that the heroic figure has always been articulated through ideological frameworks holding currency in the culture. They trace the development of separate spheres of popular culture for boys and girls to the Victorian period and argue that the rise of gender-specific literatures was supported by other cultural institutions such as the Boy Scouts and Girl Guides. Action Man is a contemporary example offered by Jonathan Bignell in his contribution to the collection. Since Action Man circulates globally, Bignell says, he is 'a medium through which economic and ideological relationships are established. Through the medium of toys, individual human subjects are constituted as consumers of products and as consumers of ideas' (pp. 231–50). It is not Action Man or any other individual property that poses a threat to the ideal childhood but the fact that children's access to these objects is mediated by the market. The useless and precious child does not labour at producing goods but s/he is increasingly solicited as a consumer of goods.

Similar arguments circulate around children and media. Children are not supposed to be directly addressed by advertisers because their exposure to markets is supposed to be mediated by caring adults, namely their parents. In *Consuming Television: Television and Its Audiences* (1997), Bob Mullan explains how *The Mickey Mouse Club* television programme marks a watershed in television advertising to children. Quoting Stephen Kline, Mullan makes the point that the *Mickey Mouse Club* was the first instance of advertisers directly addressing children as consumers. Like so many other critics, Mullan disapproves of this practice because he does not approve of children's economic independence. Not only are innocent and precious children barred from earning an income, they are also not meant to dispose of income independently.

Nick Lee makes a similar point rather nicely in his discussion of British childhood after WWII. Childhood in the post-war years, he says, was marked by complete protection from the 'bad news' of the world. Fathers filtered the bad news of the 'sphere of production' and mothers kept children buffered from 'consumption.' Children were defended at both ends of the market by parents (Lee, 2001: 156). But, Lee argues, the balance between production and consumption changed. Somewhat ironically, while television was the ideal entertainment for the cocooned family, it also brought into the home bad news of the outside world and gave children new power by addressing them as consumers. Some of the power that children had lost when they were removed from the workforce was reinstated once they were recognized as consumers. They re-engaged with the market but from a different position. No longer producers, they are now only consumers.

The ideal childhood that has been the privilege of children from middle-class families may be more susceptible to change than other childhoods. That is to say, the lives of middle-class children may be changing most dramatically at this time. It is increasingly difficult to maintain a middle-class existence on one income, and at the same time the number of sole-parent households is growing. Middle-class families are now using childcare services in greater numbers than ever before. By definition, in advanced capitalist societies all aspects of culture are sensitive to market forces and children's popular culture is no exception. Although 'the child' was brought back into the care and protection of the family home in the seventeenth century, this arrangement is by no means a perpetual one.

Public funding and childcare in Australia

In the early 1970s the Australian federal government policies began to link provision of childcare services to women's ability to participate in the workforce. A series of legislative changes began in 1950 when the

Commonwealth Arbitration Court set the first 'female basic wage' at 75 per cent of the male basic wage. Until 1966 married women were barred from working in the Commonwealth Public Service. In 1969 the Commonwealth ruled that a policy of 'equal pay for equal work' would be implemented by 1972. The Child Care Act of 1972, coincident with the formation of the Women's Electoral Lobby, brought the federal government into the provision of childcare services.

The Child Care Act of 1972 was, however, only a first step. The Act only covered provision of childcare services for children under school age. Funding was allocated by application from community groups (Brennan and O'Donnell, 1986: 23). This meant that the services most likely to receive funding would be those situated in communities that were able to access the resources (capital or cultural) necessary for submission of a winning proposal – middle-class community groups. The Act did not ensure access to childcare nationwide nor did it envisage a wide range of childcare services for children beyond the age of five.

In 1973 a women's caucus of the Australian Labor Party (Labor Women's Organisation) was able to shift policy emphasis by changing the language of the party's position, so that childcare services were to 'provide community support for women to participate more fully in society' (Brennan and O'Donnell, p. 26). Childcare was thus transformed from a 'children's service' to a critical right for women. After a struggle with the Labor Women's Organisation, in 1974 the Labor Government announced a new policy whereby children's services were established nationwide. These services were to ensure children's 'physical, social and recreational needs.' From here, OSHC was initiated along with a range of other services (Brennan and O'Donnell, pp. 34–9). Unfortunately, a change of government in 1975 brought a reduction in funding for the next several years under the Fraser coalition government.[7]

In 1975, only 2.5 per cent of the budget allocation went to OSHC. Six years later this allocation had only grown to 3 per cent. The Fraser Government turned the tables by spending nearly two-thirds of the budget on services other than preschools, although not increasing the total budget sufficiently. Brennan and O'Donnell give credit to the Fraser Government for expanding the distribution of resources beyond preschool services but assert that the 'underlying philosophy of the Fraser government was that a normally functioning family either would not require child care services or would be able to buy them privately' (pp. 44–6).

A 1981 review of Commonwealth Government Functions set out to reduce public sector expenditure but surprisingly recommended that certain childcare services be quarantined from the cuts. Among these were 'centre-based and family daycare services, out-of-school-hours care and vacation programs' (Brennan and O'Donnell, p. 50). In 1983, not long after the report, the Labor Party resumed power and one of Hawke's campaign promises was a commitment to childcare as a 'right' for all families (p. 54).

Although there was substantial shift in funding strategies for childcare services during the 1980s, OSHC fared well on balance. In 1988 the National Child Care Strategy was introduced and two-thirds of the 30,000 subsidized childcare places established were reserved for OSHC. At the same time, the government continued to encourage work-based childcare that would be partially funded by employers. This idea has continually met with resistance from the private sector. Again in 1995 the number of subsidized OSHC places was increased.

With the change of government in 1996 and under the leadership of John Howard's Liberal Coalition since that election, widespread changes have been made in childcare funding. Some of these changes have effected the way families receive a subsidy for childcare costs and others have been directed at the way in which services finance their operational costs. The change that most directly affects OSHC services and their clientele is the withdrawal of operational subsidies and the shift to the current Child Care Benefit (CCB) scheme. Operational subsidies were lump sum grants to services, but in 1997 such subsidies to OSHC services were cut and instead families were given Child Care Assistance or the Cash Rebate for OSHC. Rather than funding the provider to operate a service, the government funded the individual consumer by paying for a share of the costs to use the services. In 2000 the two systems were merged into the current CCB scheme. Under this system individual services are allowed to set their own rates and families receive a rebate from the federal government based on the family income. Allowances for more than one child in care, however, have also been cut so that the maximum rebate a family now receives is only slightly adjusted for the number of children they have in care.

These changes are seen as part of a larger movement within the Australian political right to reduce the social welfare benefit budget and to privatize enterprises like childcare. For OSHC, the last ten years of childcare 'reform' has forced services to operate more like businesses with a concern for the bottom line and to seek a balance between fees for services and meeting operational costs. Without an operational subsidy, a service is restricted to operating within the budget provided by client fees. Under the current system, services with the greatest attendance are most viable, or most likely to operate in the black.

Hourly or sessional fees for OSHC are set by individual services and vary somewhat among them. The CCB paid directly to families subsidizes the cost. For a family to qualify for the CCB, one parent or guardian must be an Australian resident, and have financial responsibility for the childcare costs of a child attending an 'approved' childcare service, and they must show compliance with immunization requirements for the child. The CCB extends to childcare services including family day care (where childcare is provided in a private home), long day care (a childcare centre usually for preschool children), occasional care (drop-in childcare), in-home care (services provided when a child is confined to the home or the family lives in a remote area without other care provisions, or where parents' work shifts that fall outside other care provision), and OSHC.

An 'approved' childcare provider is any service that meets the national standards set by the federal government which include compliance with state regulation or licensing for standards of care and facilities, staff qualifications, and participation in a quality assurance process. Operators and employees must not have criminal records or a history of bad business dealings. Although currently South Australia does not have any licensing requirements for OSHC services, the state government requires that services operating on public school grounds meet the national standards. As noted in the previous chapter, in South Australia most OSHC services operate on school grounds but this is not the case nationwide. In New South Wales, for example, town and city councils often operate services and these may or may not be located on school grounds. In Victoria, on the other hand, there is considerable provision by private enterprise. Sometimes these private providers operate their services at schools and pay a fee to the school for facility use. It seems that there is less variation in service provision within South Australia because services have maintained their ties with state government by virtue of the fact that so many services are located on public school grounds and thus come under the broad umbrella of the state.

A family receives the CCB as an immediate fee reduction at the time of service. The actual benefit (fee reduction) is calculated on the family's adjusted, taxable income (see Figure 2.1). OSHC fee is currently figured as sessional rates, per child. In the six services visited for this study, a session (3 hours and 15 minutes) for one child ranges from $7.00 to $12.00 but the average is $9.75 (at the time of publication). Using this average figure for our example, if a child attends five sessions of after-school care per week, the bill totals $48.75. The benefit in fee reduction can be as much as $35/week.

Annual Family Income	CCB per week
$45,000	$35.20
$60,000	$27.23
$80,000	$16.61
$120,000	$6.86

Figure 2.1   Child Care Benefit to family with one child attending five OSHC sessions per week (*Centrelink* Family and Child Care Services Branch, personal communication)

The CCB is a rather complicated system that makes adjustments for multiple children and gives higher benefit to preschool childcare costs but these examples give an indication of the fee reduction available. The federal income tax system also gives allowance for childcare expenditure through the Family Tax Benefits, which are generally claimed annually as part of the income tax return and extend mainly to low-income families (www.facsia.gov.au/childcarehandbook).

Participation in childcare: Who attends?

There are two systems in Australia that claim to account for childcare use. The Australian Bureau of Statistics (ABS), in its national census, collects data from families on use of childcare. The government's Department of Family and Community Services (FaCS) also conducts a survey of childcare services and issues a report called the 'Census of Child Care Services.' The two bodies use different collection methods and report their findings differently. Examining data from both reports we get a fairly good estimate of how services are used by families. In both cases, 'childcare' is the term applied to federally subsidized care for children under the age of 14. Preschool is not included because that terminology is reserved for privately funded or state-funded school preparation programmes. Although many childcare services do provide educational programmes, they are not part of the schooling system and thus are deemed to be childcare, a community service rather than an extension of the educational system.

According to ABS figures from 2002, 49 per cent of children under the age of 12 participated in some type of childcare. The most common type of *formal care* for school-aged children (from 5 to 14 years of age) was before- or after-school care, attended by 9 per cent of Australian children. Use of childcare was also positively correlated with higher family income. For all children, use of all forms of childcare was higher for those whose parents were employed. In families where both parents work, 59 per cent of children used childcare. If only one parent worked, 35 per cent attend childcare, and where both parents were unemployed, only 28 per cent of children participated in childcare. For children from single-parent families, the use of care was even higher. 74 per cent of children with their sole parent employed used care, compared with 44 per cent of children whose sole parent was not employed.

Vacation Care use is even higher than before- and after-school care for all groups. 17 per cent of children living with two parents who are both employed used Vacation Care. In families where the sole parent was employed, the figure is higher: 27 per cent (ABS Report 4402.0). Although the ABS figures do not always distinguish among types of childcare, their reports do indicate a positive correlation between childcare use and employment.

The most recent publication from FaCS is the '2002 Census of Child Care Services' (www.facs.gov.au). Employees within South Australia's DECS claim that FaCS data reflect a more accurate account of childcare in Australia. According to this report, we can estimate that 15 per cent of primary school children in South Australia attend OSHC. The estimate is calculated from the total number of children between the ages of 5 and 14 residing in the state. This is the age bracket issued by the national census although its inclusion of children between the ages of 12 and 14 means that its base includes children who would be beyond the age bracket of OSHC. Without an accurate census for the OSH C-specific age bracket, we can only estimate the percentage of children utilizing the service. In a state with a population just under 1.5 million people, we do know that 17,500 attend OSHC (before- and/or after-school care) and 12,400 attend Vacation Care during school holidays. Another complicating factor in the methods used by census takers is that they do not detail whether the children attending Vacation Care are the same children who attend OSHC during the regular school term. It is most likely that these two populations overlap. If a parent's daily work schedule normally coincides with the school schedule, after-school care may not be utilized, but Vacation Care may be necessary during school holidays. Some parents choose to take their annual leave when children are also on school breaks and those who might regularly use before- or after-school care might not attend Vacation Care services.

The FaCS data confirm the ABS findings and specify for South Australia that childcare is more often used by parents in the workforce. FaCS report for South Australia that 69 per cent of children in OSHC attend because both parents work, while 27 per cent attend because their sole parent works. Working parents thus account for more than 90 per cent of the children's attendance at OSHC.

OSHC in South Australia – Childcare, not schooling

Changing adult work patterns coupled with a growing concern to ensure child safety helped drive the development of OSHC services in the late twentieth century. If there is a social stigma attached to attending OSHC, even greater disfavour is brought upon parents of so-called latchkey children. Sometimes generated by child advocacy groups and often circulated and popularized in media reports, concerns about children who spend their after-school hours at home without adult supervision include the view that children will idle away their time, neglecting home work or activities that are deemed worthwhile. It is feared that these children will not get physical exercise, but will instead consume 'empty calories' while sitting and watching TV or playing video games. Even more disturbing is the belief that unsupervised children will come to harm at the hands of strangers. Children don't even walk to and from school any more because adults fear that children may come to harm in open and public spaces.

Network of Community Activities, a leading Australian not-for-profit organization and advocate for OSHC services, has mobilized such views in their newsletter:

> increasingly the local neighbourhood is seen as hostile and dangerous. Parents understandably are reluctant to allow children to play unattended, the local corner store may have been replaced by a regional shopping centre, streets have become dangerous thoroughfares and dezoning of schools has led to fragmentation of neighbourhood networks all leading to decreasing opportunities for school age children to play independently and safely.
>
> (1993: 3)

The growth of OSHC has been stimulated by such unsavoury views of public space coupled with increased workforce participation and the rise in single-parent families.

According to the ABS figures quoted above, it is the children of middle-class families who appear to be using OSHC services most. Given this fact, it is not surprising that the ideal middle-class childhood upon which OSHC models its services is accepted without question. Ironically, if the experience of the ideal childhood is still possible, for many it is only accessible through its provision by public institutions of childcare and not within children's family homes. The middle-class family relies for its existence on public services like childcare.

In South Australia, 70 per cent of OSHC services are operated on government (state) school grounds and the remainder at non-government (independent or religious) schools, community centres, and churches. Typically a service will provide a combination of indoor and outdoor space for children's play. Programmes vary with respect to facility resources but most offer a daily guided art and craft activity (making something with a set of given materials), additional space for children to pursue their own independent drawing and art making, an area with soft furnishings for relaxing, reading, and socializing, a space for building forts and playing dress up, and most have a range of board games, cars, blocks, and other children's playthings. Cooking projects are common where kitchen facilities exist, and some facilities have billiards or foosball tables. Most services also have television, video playback, video games, CD players, and some form of computer access, as well as books and magazines.

Outdoor space available to children varies with staffing and the location of the outdoor spaces relative to other spaces used by OSHC. The staffing ratio is set at a minimum of 1:15 for on-site supervision and 1:8 for excursions. Services with lower attendance rates have fewer staff and thus cannot utilize as many separate physical spaces as more heavily populated services would. This sometimes imposes a limit on the actual space that is utilized at any one time from within the overall space provided to the service by the host school or organization. Even if a service has access to an indoor play space, an outdoor play space, and a computer room, they may not be able to use all three spaces at once because with fewer than 31 children, they may only have two staff members present.

Outdoor activities often include organized games and/or sport in which an adult participates or merely observes children's play, and use of playground equipment and other facilities. With skin cancer a serious concern in Australia, many playgrounds have shade-covered areas with benches and picnic tables where children play cards, games, or practise performances under cover from the sun but still outdoors.

An after-school session normally begins by registering the attendance of children as they arrive from school (around 3.15 p.m.) and then offering a generous snack comprised from some combination of sand-wiches, cookies, cheese and crackers, and fruit. After this the children disperse to their chosen activities. Usually all the activities are on offer simultaneously, only limited by the ability of the service to staff the necessary physical spaces in which these activities occur. Children choose whether they will play outside or inside, what they will do, which friends they will play with, and for how long they will participate in any given activity.

Among the few activities that are time regulated, media play is most rigorously monitored. This is because their popularity is greater than their provision. Most services have only one television and one or two video game console set-ups, and computer access is quite varied from service to service. A service with one television, a video player and a video game console, will often alternate use of the television set as a monitor for video game playing, a screen for video playback, and a TV for watching broadcast television programming. Services that are able to utilize the school's computer facilities can often provide greater com-puter access to children. These computers are normally situated in the school's computer lab, a facility that is often located in a separate build-ing from the OSHC service. The physical location of the computer room requires that the service allocate a staff member to supervise that space, at a ratio of one adult for every 15 children. Services with small popula-tions of children have fewer staff and consequently are often unable to assign a staff member to the computer lab while maintaining sufficient supervision over the other areas of indoor and outdoor space. Staffing resources limit the time available to use computers when computers are separate from other activity areas.

In a typical afternoon session, from 3.30 p.m. to 6.00 p.m. children will be dispersed between the outdoor and indoor facilities, playing ball games and climbing on equipment, practising dance routines to music played on the CD player, playing video games on console and Game Boy, cooking, making art, reading, doing homework, and hang-ing out with their friends. Sometimes children will plan their activities around cooking because this activity is highly structured and super-vised, especially when the stove or oven is required. A large proportion of children plan their time around playing video games because a system of turn taking is made necessary by the great demand put on limited resources. Television in most services is only available from 5.00 p.m. when video games are no longer in use and staff are cleaning up in advance of the session concluding, and parents are coming by to collect children.

Media use in OSHC – A few introductory remarks

Within the recreational, leisure-time environment provided by OSHC, children's access to media is public, and its use is social. Most media play, like other forms of play at OSHC, is not conducted in isolation but among a group of friends or peers. These facts make media use in OSHC distinct from the trends developing for households. Recent surveys of children's media use in homes indicate that children are increasingly accessing media in rooms separate from the main living area, isolated from others and away from a regulatory gaze of adults. Although this study did not capture information about the location of computers, video game machines, and other media in households, children were asked about home use generally and to identify how they played with each medium so that comparisons could be drawn between OSHC and homes. (see Appendix 2, 'Interview Form').

Accounting for media provision, access, and patterns of use is easiest for classrooms. None of the children's classrooms regularly provide access to entertainment media of any type. Not surprising, broadcast television is rarely used in classrooms. Videotaped TV programmes or films are occasionally screened to elaborate upon or enrich concepts and lessons. Children from one class said that their teacher infrequently rewarded the class with a 'Friday video' and the treat would be an entertainment programme or children's film. Video game machines do not exist in classrooms, and Game Boy devices are to be securely stored during class time, if they are allowed at all. CD players are normally used for lessons and sometimes to help relax children during a rest period, but music is not generally used to enhance the mood or atmosphere of the classroom. Computer access in schools is mainly provided in the computer lab, a separate facility distinct from the regular classroom. Some classes have one or two computers and most classes have 20 to 30 students. Regular daily access to computers in classrooms is very limited.

On the surface, media provision and access in OSHC share more in common with homes than with classrooms. Despite similarities in provision and access, media use in OSHC is quite different to media use in homes. So, on the one hand, the provision of media is like homes but, on the other hand, its use is not. If we are to understand the range of media access and patterns of use that children deploy in their everyday encounters with media, knowledge of what children do with media in OSHC is critical. Recognizing the unique opportunities that the OSHC context provides, we can structure after-school care environments in ways that will support children's efforts to become self-managing in their media use.

The interviews with children generated valuable indicators about the forms and quantity of media in each household and about the ways children use these media in the different spaces of home, classroom, and OSHC (see Figure 2.2). The data reflected in this study suggest that a finer-grain analysis should be pursued in future studies but the information provided here was not available elsewhere at the time the study commenced. This study establishes a base from which we can launch further research to discover finer distinctions.

Although the home inventory of media did not account for music-listening devices, girls often listen to CDs at OSHC while choreographing and rehearsing performances set to popular music. At two services researchers questioned the girls as to whether they invented the dance routines or were imitating performances they had seen elsewhere. They did both. Imitating music video dance routines at OSHC is an example of how media knowledge migrates with the child between the spaces of home and OSHC because they do not watch music videos at OSHC. Whether the routines were mimicked or originally choreographed, the generic knowledge of music videos comes from experiences outside OSHC and demonstrates that children can be

---

- Fewer children play video games at OSHC than at home

- Less than half the girls who reported playing video games at home also played at OSHC

- Among boys, almost all (89 per cent) played video games at home and OSHC

- Boys more often reported having game machines at home and even those without access at home played video games at OSHC

- More children play video games alone at home

- At OSHC children play video games with partners or in groups

- Most children watch TV regularly at home while less than half said they watch TV at OSHC

- Video-tape viewing in OSHC closely matches the frequency reported for home use

---

Figure 2.2   Media use at home and at OSHC

inspired to imaginative and physical play by the media performances they have seen on television.[8]

In early 2000 the ABS had not yet published their findings on children's leisure-time pursuits. Thus, our interviews were conducted without reference to surveys that have since been published by ABS. A 'Survey of Children's Participation in Culture and Leisure Activities' (ABS, cat. no. 4901.0) has been conducted in 2000, 2003, and 2006. The survey details the involvement of children aged 5 to 14 years in leisure activities outside school. The key findings on media include: 'a noticeable change in children playing computer games which decreased by 4 percentage points from 71% in 2000 to 67% in 2006' and,

> a significant increase in the percentage of South Australian children accessing the Internet between 2000 and 2003 (from 49% in 2000 to 66% in 2003). In 2006, 65% of children accessed the Internet. Conversely, the percentage of children using a computer but not accessing the Internet decreased from 50% in 2000 to 30% in 2003 and 2006.
>
> (ABS, 4901.0, 2006)

These findings point to greater Internet connectivity in family homes associated with a broadband boom.

Most interestingly, in a section called, 'Other Leisure Activities,' it is reported that

> In the two weeks leading up to the [2006] survey, the three most popular leisure activities for South Australian children aged 5–14 years were watching TV, videos or DVDs (98%), reading for pleasure (73%) and playing electronic or computer games (67%). It is interesting to note that South Australian children were more commonly involved in reading for pleasure than playing electronic or computer games. While similar proportions of boys and girls watch TV, videos or DVDs (98% for both), more boys than girls play computer or electronic games than girls (83% compared with 51%) while more girls than boys do art and craft (63% compared with 40%), as well as reading for pleasure (77% compared with 68%).
>
> (ABS, 4901.0, 2006)

It appears that 'old media' are still important to children's lives with TV and reading ahead of computer game playing when both boys and girls are accounted for. The respectable position of reading for pleasure may also be due in part to the Premier's Reading Challenge (http://www.premiersreadingchallenge.sa.edu.au/prc). The statewide initiative was launched in 2004 as a way to promote reading for pleasure among school children.

In the next chapter I explain how OSHC is an intermediary space that triangulates with the well-studied domains of home and classroom. Understanding the mediating role that OSHC serves between home and classroom helps us situate findings like those outlined above and appreciate some of the more complex media use patterns and arrangements that we commonly see when children's media use is public, social, and recreational.

3
Intermediary Space

It seems to be well established that physical space has no 'reality' without the energy that is deployed within it.
—Henri Lefebvre, 1974: 13

A social space cannot be adequately accounted for either by nature (climate, site) or by its previous history ... Mediations, and mediators, have to be taken into consideration: the action of groups, factors within knowledge, within ideology, within the domain of representations.
—Henri Lefebvre, 1974: 77

Theorizing OSHC as intermediary space

Out of School Hours Care (OSHC) is first and foremost a social space. It is a place where children meet and pursue recreational or leisure-time activities. Among these activities, media play features prominently and is one of the most popular pastimes. But OSHC, and the sort of media play that goes on there, is part of a child's larger social world, which includes home life and the routines of schooling in an advanced capitalist society. Electronic media and ICT exist in all three of these arenas and they connect these places in unique ways. They are among the mediators that Lefebvre would have us consider when seeking to understand the 'energy' of a social space. Media play in OSHC is therefore mediated by influences from the larger social sphere that, for most children, includes home and classroom most prominently. Children bring to OSHC their knowledge and practices of media that are in part generated in the spaces of home and classroom. To understand how

61

knowledge about media migrates across the borders that separate these three spaces and, more particularly, how OSHC mediates between home and classroom, this chapter addresses the intermediary nature of OSHC and the mediating functions it serves.

Characterizing OSHC as intermediary space allows us to account for physical, temporal, and ideological dimensions of mediation and the manner in which a child orients himself or herself to electronic entertainment and ICT. Explicitly, the way OSHC mediates a child's time is evident in the OSHC nomenclature: before-school care, after-school care, and Vacation Care. Before and after class time and in between school terms, the academic timetable of days and sessions is linked by definition to these childcare services. Children attend OSHC at specified times of day, in the morning before school starts or in the afternoon before going home. The chronology of a child's day or week can be mediated by attendance at OSHC. Although many children attend after-school care daily, others come only on particular days of the week. For some children, those who live between two homes in shared custody arrangements for instance, a week with one parent may be marked by attendance at OSHC: 'I only get to come here when it's my Mum's week,' one child lamented to me.

The intermediary nature of OSHC is also evident spatially in the use of physical space. OSHC is a particular place and it physically mediates between home and school because it is *the place* children 'go to' before or after school, on the way to the classroom or en route home. Although most services operate on school grounds, they use school space in quite different ways to classrooms and this proves to be very interesting for the ways in which spatial use influences or shapes media play. The use of physical space has consequences for the social dimensions of media use and for the ways in which children can use their bodies in media play.

In an ideological sense as well, OSHC services are intermediary spaces. The rules and regulations that govern social activity in OSHC – and media use is a social activity – are often quite different from those experienced at home or at school. For instance, because OSHC services strive to meet the needs and desires of all the children in attendance, they often use a popular vote to make decisions about which game to play first or which video to watch. Such democratic process is distinct from many family homes and certainly most classrooms, where adult agendas and authority rule. While media play in OSHC is shaped by the rules of use within each service, regulation from outside OSHC also exerts some influence. OSHC is a place where the different sets of rules and regulations that govern media use at home and in school are negotiated by children and adults.

Since OSHC differs from home and classrooms physically, temporally, and ideologically, it not only operates differently but also feels different. Affectively, OSHC is experienced by children as a unique place. It is in this sense that Sony's notion of 'third place' provides an appropriate short hand for OSHC and helps us focus on media play within this context.

The sense with which I use the term 'third place' is borrowed from Sony's PlayStation2 marketing campaign. Sony's 'third place' is not a real place but a virtual one, created by media and mediation. Sony claimed, during the marketing campaign for PS2 that, their technology creates a third place. We should expect nothing less from a marketing and advertising campaign, but there is more to this notion of third place than the technological dimension. As a community constituted in place, OSHC mediates between homes and classrooms. The way we describe OSHC and even the way we define it, 'before-school' and 'after-school' care, suggests that OSHC orbits school like the planets spin around the sun. In its nomenclature, time and OSHC, are defined by the school day. But, for children and their everyday lives, OSHC is experienced alongside school and home as part of the fuller routine of a day or a week. Once we begin to view OSHC as equal with school in importance to children's every day lived experience, we can imagine a triangle that links the three places, home, classroom, and OSHC. From this perspective, the dyadic and linear view of children's time–space occupation is inadequate; a multi-dimensional image of how time and space are related becomes more evident. A simple opposition between home and classroom is not possible when the third place of OSHC is introduced. Between home and classroom, the movement of bodies and bodies of knowledge are mediated by OSHC. Recognizing the significance of the third place adds a complication to our neat division of children's media as either entertaining or educational. The third place, OSHC, is a perfect location for the boundary-blurring concept of 'Edutainment,' the idea that education and entertainment are conceptually linked.

Even though OSHC services are most often located on school sites and are thus subject to standards of safety and certain social norms of schooling, they differ from school with respect to how time is utilized. At OSHC children do not have to keep pace with the rigorous temporal segmentation typical of a school day's lesson structure. In primary schooling, for example, classroom lessons are structured in 10-, 15-, and 20-minute activity blocks, with time periods increasing with the children's age or year in school. In OSHC, time is not segmented or blocked in this manner but is experienced more fluidly. Children have more autonomy over how they structure their time around the given activities. Arts and crafts activities and materials may be available for one and half hours, and a child may spend as long or little time at that activity as s/he pleases, coming and going between other activities. At services which provide Internet access, children can browse their favourite website, even if the site is not related to their studies. Children can use the craft materials provided for an art project to create an entirely different object than the one given as an example. In OSHC, there is a greater degree of freedom for children to use the provided materials in an individually inspired manner than in classrooms because the OSHC space is a recreational one and the activities are child centred rather than adult directed at a micro-level. In other words, at OSHC activity rather than output, process rather than product, is emphasized. And, unlike classrooms, the goals in OSHC are set by children and not by adults. OSHC, as noted earlier, is a site for informal learning where children set the agenda; pursue their interests at their pace, with their friends; and the output of their activities is not assessed or evaluated.

In part, the differences in the way time is used at school and at OSHC are generated by the commitment OSHC maintains to providing children with a play space. Given this fundamental philosophy, we have to ask, what about children's play distinguishes it from other childhood activities. What are our understandings and expectations of children's play? Brian Sutton-Smith's ideas on play are useful here. Sutton-Smith (1997) identifies a fundamental 'ambiguity of play.' On the one hand, children's play is often observed as having little to do with anything else, as being carnivalesque. On the other hand, play 'is typically interpreted as having value not just for itself but because of other functions that it serves in individual development and group culture.' This fundamental contradiction persists in generating opposing views of play. Sutton-Smith argues that 'The desire for children to make progress in development and schooling has led to play's being considered either as a waste of time (the view of educational "conservatives") or a form of children's work (the belief of educational "progressives"). The one view is that play is not usefully adaptive, the other that it is' (p. 19). But the concept of edutainment brings these two views together and this, I would argue, makes adults uncomfortable. It is difficult to accept that children's play is complex, that it is more than meets the eye, or that its value may be undetectable to adults. The slipperiness of a concept like edutainment makes it difficult to grasp. Where does education end and entertainment begin?

After-school-hours care often becomes embroiled in the contradiction that is ascribed to edutainment because it straddles two worldviews about what constitutes appropriate recreation and leisure for children. On the one hand, children are granted time and space to play. On the other hand, that play is often criticized if it is not productive. Media play in particular is often characterized as mindless entertainment and sometimes even as detrimental to children's development.

The imperative for after-school hours to be productive time is common in the US where after-school-hours care has only been funded as a necessary social service in economically poor communities and, more recently, where academic achievement is low and children are perceived to be at risk for crime, either as perpetrators or victims (see Chapter 2). For these children, and poor children in general, after-school programmes often provide compensatory educational programmes and little play. Children who do not meet the requisite achievement standard at school are not granted leisure time for play outside school. Children are expected to complete the 'job' of learning before they can claim leisure time in which to pursue recreational activities. Robert Halpern (2003) says of after-school programmes in the US that they have

> often stood – or found themselves – at the intersection of ideological crosscurrents in American society: between romantic and instrumental views of children, between play and work, between the traditions of local communities and those of the larger society, and between a view of low-income children as vulnerable and a view of them as threatening.
>
> (pp. 2–3)

Throughout the 1990s, Halpern says, 'the preoccupation with efficient and productive time use that defined adult life in American culture spread to childhood, and to the out-of-school hours.' This, he says, gave rise to two sets of concerns: that unsupervised play might be useless play or 'a lost opportunity' and that this time could be better utilized helping children to raise their literacy levels, since school time did not seem to be achieving this goal sufficiently (pp. 91–2).

In Australia, however, there is no comparable sense of crisis surrounding children's school achievement and life is more *leisurely* for adults and children. A rich leisure life and public provision of services supporting leisure pursuits in Australia are not simple rhetoric. Swimming lessons, public playing fields and sporting facilities, adult leisure and recreation courses, cultural events and centres are all subsidized by government investment and reasonably accessed and utilized by the public. Play is generally viewed as what children do and, to a lesser extent, as a learning experience in itself. There is no momentum to extend the school day, and OSHC is generally not called upon to provide anything other than a safe and pleasant recreational experience. These views inform the Australian provision of OSHC and more closely parallel children's own views of play, as described by Sutton-Smith. He says children understand play as 'having fun, being outdoors, being with friends, choosing freely, not working, pretending, enacting, fantasy and drama, and playing games' (1997: 49). At OSHC children are allowed the autonomy to 'choose freely' from among the activities on offer and to decide for themselves when they will shift from one activity to another. In this way, their experience of time in OSHC is quite different from their experience of time in classrooms where curriculum, teachers, and timetables set the pace and duration of activities.

Stanley Parker (1976) has argued in a similar vein about the more far-reaching term, leisure. 'It is doubtful,' he writes, 'whether we can sensibly use the concept of leisure at all for pre-school children, since time for them has not become institutionally divided between obligatory activity (at school) and non-obligatory activity. For school children the notion of leisure becomes more appropriate ...' (p. 51). Rather than defining leisure as the opposite of work, Parker says that it is more productive to recognize that 'leisure behaviour is subjective, and is satisfying and desirable to the extent that it is freely chosen' (p. 133). Parker says,

> Our schools, colleges and universities are organized on the implicit assumption that the educational task is primarily to prepare young people for a career, or at least a means of earning a living. The emphasis is on school *work* rather than on school *leisure*.
>
> (p. 91)

When schools do participate in education of leisure, Parker says it is usually with an emphasis on 'high culture arts' rather than 'entertainment' (Parker, p. 93). As an example, Parker says schools disparage contemporary popular music of a commercial nature and prefer to offer instruction in folk or classical traditions. He attributes such elitist leanings of most school-based education for leisure to the 'long and sometimes noble history of efforts to "improve" other people' (p. 96). Some would argue that this characterization does not apply to Australian schooling, that Australian schools do not emphasize high-culture training. Some would even argue that for young countries with powerful mythologies of middle-class culture, such as Australia and the US, there is no tradition of high art. Putting aside the more far-reaching implications of this debate, it is certainly true that neither Australian nor American classrooms have video game machines, and the use of television or video programming is almost exclusive to carefully selected content that supports a curriculum unit. As far as popular media are concerned, schools do not generally value television, video games, movies, and trading cards for their content or the activities that circulate through them (Hodge and Tripp, 1986).

When asked whether they ever watched television in their classrooms, many children answered with a tone of disappointment or disdain that they had seen the Olympic Games Opening Ceremonies or science programmes relevant to their studies. The most emotionally positive recollection was given by a few of these children who said that they had watched the movie *A Bug's Life* when the class studied insects. This was exceptional and upholds Hodge and Tripp's findings from the mid-1980s that classrooms are not TV-friendly places. It is safe to say that, for children, access to entertainment media is associated with leisure time, whether or not children actually distinguish leisure from other forms of activity. Moreover, children know which forms of media are acceptable in each domain: the classroom, at home, and elsewhere.

Inspired by Hodge and Tripp's earlier research, Ellen Seiter (1999) has looked at the regulation of video and television in preschool (childcare) settings because

> Problems around television viewing in institutional settings reflect the ambiguous definition of these childcare spaces as intermediaries between the home (where television viewing is usually frequent and acceptable) and school (where explicit learning, rather than merely child care, is supposed to be taking place).
>
> (p. 239)

Seiter examines how media use is emblematic of physical and temporal intermediation and she identifies ideological and chronological components of intermediation. She does not, however, theorize this intermediation as occurring simultaneously across time and space dimensions. She looks at preschool as a chronological moment in a child's life: attending preschool occurs at a stage in a child's life, between the more individually oriented infant care and the more institutionalized primary school years. Seiter describes preschool as intermediary in three ways. Firstly, it exists in a physical space distinct from home and school. Secondly, it exists to serve a chronological imperative, as the 'pre' of preschool suggests. Third, she demonstrates how both these dimensions contribute to a set of ideological functions that mediate between the regimes of home life and primary schooling.

Although indebted to the insights provided by Seiter and Hodge and Tripp, I am amplifying their work and varying the emphasis at the same time. Like Hodge and Tripp, I am concerned with school-aged children who, on the whole, are better able to speak for themselves than are pre-school children. While Hodge and Tripp maintained the binary divide between home and school, the nature and mandate of OSHC challenge such a duality. Instead of accepting the division between home and classroom, I am looking for the ways in which OSHC connects these spaces and closes the gap between them.

For Seiter, the idea of intermediation accounts for the significance of a place (childcare) at a critical moment in a child's life – the years before the child enters formal schooling. The intermediary character and function of OSHC cannot be isolated in this way, as a chronological moment in time, because children may attend OSHC for several years as they move through primary schooling. The OSHC population is also more heterogeneous than a preschool population. Children at OSHC range in age from 5 to 12 years. Because children in South Australia do not have to attend their local school, they may also come from widely varied backgrounds. This situation is less likely in a preschool where children attend close to home or close to a parent's place of employment (both of which are more economically and socially homogeneous than many Australian public schools). Among the sites included in this study are two that serve school populations where nearly 50 per cent of the children are from immigrant families, newcomers to Australia.[1]

I am looking at the synchronic features of temporality: a child attends school, lives in a family, and attends OSHC, all within the same chrono-logical period of life. Taking this position has consequences for how ide-ological intermediation is constructed and accounted for. Since OSHC is coeval, or exists in the same time frame, with home and school, the ide-ological work of OSHC exists alongside ideologies generated in home and classroom settings. To adequately account for children's acquisition of media competency we must consider the simultaneous influence of intermediary spaces because they exist alongside and not independent of other influences and instruction from classroom and/or home. Knowledge of media resides with the individual and is reflected in the mobility of the individual across and between spaces. What is learned and practised at home informs activities elsewhere and vice versa. Children's media experiences in OSHC do not exist independent of their media experiences in classrooms or at home, but, rather, in relation to those other experiences.

With respect to a child's media competency, the emphasis on simultaneity is important because recreational use of media, like media play in OSHC, may have consequences for more formal uses of media. By formal uses of media I mean the application of media skills to facilitate studies and work. Informal learning about media use often occurs as a consequence of a different and more explicit goal: playing a game well, for instance, or text messaging a friend about a social event. For children and adults, a great deal of our media knowledge is acquired in this informal fashion through the activities that constitute a community of practice around other activities. When using email or instant messaging systems to communicate for social purposes, an individual practises media skills that can be used in other contexts, more formal contexts like work.

Drawing on a survey of 480 students, interviews with their parents, and findings from friendship-based focus groups, Sarah L. Holloway and Gill Valentine (2001) have found that children's use of ICT at home differs from their use of ICT at school. The authors attribute this to the differences between adult–child relations at home and peer relations at school.

> These discourses about adult-child differences were important in the home where technology emerged as a symbol of the future. However, in negotiating their technical competence in school, children rarely identify themselves as belonging to the (homogenous group 'child', and instead draw on other discourses about technology – particularly the ways in which it is gendered through its association with marginal masculinity – to understand and mark the differences between themselves and their peers. In this context, technology emerges as a signifier of social inadequacy rather than as a symbol of the future, and children thus construct technical competence in much less favourable ways at school than in the domestic context.
>
> (p. 35)

Holloway and Valentine have shown how children's communities of practice in school and home construct different social values for children's competence with ICT. These social values result in different uses of ICT in the two distinct places. They argue that the use of ICT in each place is 'shaped by the socio-spatial relations which constitute "the" home and "the" school' (2001: 26). The social meaning that is ascribed to ICT in each environment influences how the technologies are used in those particular places. What emerges from their study is a view of girls performing their technical competence *only* at home and not at school because in school they are socially penalized by their peers if they appear to be 'computer geeks.'

In earlier work (Vered, 1998b) I have noted a related phenomenon among primary school girls who were quite skilled and knowledgeable about computer games from their home play experiences but were reluctant to play these games at school. I attributed this to gender politics and the dynamics of play in a gender-mixed environment. For young girls it may be that they do not like to play with boys or by the rules boys set, as I concluded in that earlier study. For older girls it may be that they do not want to bear a mark of masculinity, labelled as a computer geek, as Holloway and Valentine suggest. In both studies, however, recreational use of computers was linked with school use of computers and girls opted-out of some school activities. Although for the older girls their informal use of computers was quite high, they withdrew from some of the formal uses of computers associated with school. The young girls that I studied did not withdraw from the formal computer activities of the classroom but they did shy away from the recreational uses of the computer at school where boys dominated the equipment and set a raucous tone.

Children, especially girls, with computers at home have a great advantage over children without home access. Although researchers have identified how parental belief in children's technical ability benefits some girls, providing them with a way to challenge the school-based construction of girls as technically inept, they do not suggest how we might foster similarly positive cultural constructions in places outside the home (Holloway & Valentine, 2001: 36). A logical recommendation might be to call for placement of more computers in public recreational centres where the positive benefits of recreational computer use might be extended to children who do not have home access. Computers in public places might generate communities of practice around a shared interest in entertainment objects and thereby bring together highly skilled and novice users around the nexus of entertainment, with consequences for overall media competency and skills acquisition.

Holloway and Valentine's research points to the importance of place, and we can infer that the specific ways in which young children use electronic media in the particular space of OSHC is important to the development of media competency and identity. Following Holloway and Valentine we might ask, what are the socio-spatial relations that constitute OSHC and how do they shape media use in OSHC and elsewhere?

Can positive relations with ICT in OSHC have consequences for ICT use in classrooms and elsewhere? What are the forces at play in OSHC that help shape children's identities as media consumers and producers?

OSHC sites are points of intersection between home and school and thus places in which mediation occurs, but they are also places with unique structures and regulatory schemes all their own. For instance, how does the democratic imperative – voting on which video to watch – influence a child's perception of media use in OSHC and how does it affect their views of media use elsewhere? In a classroom, when a film, video or television programme is shown, the teacher usually chooses what the children will watch. In some families who gets to select a video from the shop is alternated among the siblings and adults, while in others the children decide jointly and unanimously. For the single-child family, selecting a video may not involve any compromise. Since a majority of Australian households have more than one television, even in larger families children may be able to select a video without having to negotiate with siblings or parents. In OSHC, however, scarce resources and large numbers of children mean that compromise is the norm. Most services have only one television and one VCR. Children usually have to agree on the video selection because the resource base is not sufficient for individual choice to be indulged. Use of media in OSHC is regulated, to a large degree, by circumstances rather than policy. OSHC has no explicit policy about media provision, access, or use. Services are warned about copyright regulations regarding public performances, which is mainly applicable to video (DVD) use in OSHC. In South Australia, OSHC services are supposed to follow the guidelines for media use in schooling. They do not, however, follow these guidelines very closely. One aim of this research has been to inform the development of policy guidelines for media use in OSHC which will address its particular nature and encourage a positive approach to leisure-time use of media.

After-school clubs in England and Wales have been characterized by geographers Fiona Smith and John Barker (2000) as intermediary space and sometimes as contested space. One of their aims has been to document children's use of space in after-school clubs because after-school clubs are relatively new in England and, as such, research on them is sparse. A similar situation is found in Australia, where OSHC is the least studied and least well-documented segment of the childcare industry, although it has been publicly funded since 1986, and is currently the fastest growing sector of the childcare industry. Studies of media access and use in OSHC are scarce. In response to the situation in Britain, Smith and Barker set out to 'explore some of the ways in which children's sense of place in the out of school club links the material environment to the meanings they attribute to it' (2000: 315).

They determined that after-school clubs in their study could be characterized as 'contested spaces' where children are at odds with the adult sensibility responsible for defining the space and the exercise of adult power through surveillance and regulation. They demonstrate how children in highly structured and regulated spaces, in which there are right and wrong ways to play in space, seek to subvert control, transgress boundaries, and generally avoid being caught by mechanisms of surveillance. They link such behaviour to 'the importance of space and place to the continuous restructuring of power and identity' (Smith and Barker, 2000: 315). By extension, their work suggests that media use in OSHC is also important for the negotiation of power and identity because media are part of the material and cultural environment of not only OSHC but also home, school, and society, more broadly. Knowledge of media and popular entertainment provide valuable cultural capital that can be deployed in the processes of identity formation. The communities of practice that develop around media objects, like fan-culture practices, are fertile beds for the formation of identity and assertions of identity (Buckingham and Sefton-Green, 2003).

Unfortunately, very little in the description of British after-school clubs, provided by Smith and Barker, is paralleled in South Australian OSHC services. This is in part a result of the differences between the British and Australian programmes, but it is also reflective of differences in the research agendas between their study and this one. In their 15-page article on 'contested space,' Smith and Barker devote two sentences to media: 'Older children's rooms were equipped with pool tables, stereos, dart boards and televisions. Videos and computer games were also common, with films and games deemed unsuitable for younger children' (2000: 327). For media studies scholarship, Smith and Barker's goal (to understand 'the ways in which children's sense of place in the out of school club links the material environment to the meanings they attribute to it' (p. 315)) can be examined quite productively by looking at how media play is situated within the context of all play at OSHC. Elsewhere, Smith and Barker note that while sofas in the TV area were meant to replicate a homey feeling with the clubs, children

> actively rejected a construction [of the club] that drew upon and reflected discourses associated with the domestic sphere. Children appeared to enjoy the specificity and uniqueness of the out of school

club, rather than its similarity with, or connection to, the home environment.

(Smith and Barker, 2002: 67)

The distinction that children in the British study are asserting is not in conflict with the findings for South Australia. What is different though is the apparent need to assert this distinction. OSHC services in South Australia are already constructed as unique spaces, different from home and classroom, and children's knowledge of media use rules respects these distinctions.

Most of the children interviewed for this study were easily able to explain that OSHC only allowed G and PG classified movies, and many gave examples of the different rules between home and OSHC specific to video game play. Children with siblings offered several versions of what is best described as 'keep your hands to yourself,' as a rule that applies to video game play at home. At OSHC, in contradistinction, most video game play is group play and helping others is common (see Figure 3.1).

Figure 3.1   Children playing video games together

OSHC services in South Australia appear to be doing what Smith and Barker recommend, that is taking children's 'views and wishes' seriously, sometimes to the point that OSHC media policies challenge those of the school rather than reinforce them and, similarly, vary from practices in individual family homes.

Domestic disruptions

OSHC provides a unique place where some of the rules about media use at home and school can be circumvented, negotiated, and reinvented for the purposes of OSHC culture. Owing to the high cost of Game Boy devices and the possibility of some children misplacing such small items, some schools (and parents) do not allow the hand-held video games at school. (One school in the study maintained a total ban on Pokemon and thus did not allow Game Boy devices that came from the factory with the Pokemon logo.) OSHC, however, generally allows these playthings to be brought from home. Many OSHC services have their own Game Boys. Children can use OSHC Game Boy cartridges or bring their own from home. Bringing a Game Boy cartridge from home and sharing or swapping at OSHC shows how the space can provide an opportunity to disrupt the insulation of the home and its regulatory scheme, as well as to circumvent the school's prohibitions.

An example of disruption occurred at a service in a working class community, when a Game Boy cartridge was loaned between children at OSHC, but the borrower *'forgot'* to return the game to the lending child. The incident prompted 'a serious chit chat' between OSHC staff and the children. The children were lectured on the value of these games: they were reminded that the games are expensive, and that having Game Boys available at OSHC is a privilege. The discussion clearly framed Game Boy use at OSHC in terms of parental concern for property, the material value or cost of the devices, and how access is shaped by these facts.

In this case, OSHC staff were made to mediate between home and public, to intervene between child and parent, to make the values of some families a public concern. While OSHC can serve as a marketplace for the exchange of games beyond the reach of parental control, when the transaction does not run smoothly, parents may expect that their values will be asserted and upheld by OSHC staff.

Parents also use OSHC and its media as a form of leverage within the household. Children are often reluctant to go home when the parent arrives in the middle of an important activity, such as a turn at the video game. On several occasions during the research, I overheard parents bribing their children to come home with the offer of media: 'If you come right now I'll hire that game from the shop for the weekend.' At the opposite end of the spectrum, some parents use media deprivation at OSHC as a punishment for transgressions that have occurred elsewhere. Parents will send children to OSHC with instructions that they are forbidden to use the video games at OSHC because they have been naughty at home. OSHC staff particularly dislike these directives because it puts the burden of enforcement on them and makes OSHC the site of punishment when the 'crime,' as it were, has had nothing to do with the child's behaviour at OSHC. OSHC staff do not like having the responsibility of disciplinary enforcement foisted upon them and they object to participating in a system that potentially may colour the child's attitude towards the OSHC experience. OSHC staff typically respond to such parental pressure by assuming that it is the child's responsibility to follow parental instructions and they distance themselves from the practice.

Whither the private/public divide?

Studies of children's media use in intermediary spaces like OSHC can help to demonstrate how social and material changes are posing a significant challenge to the dominant paradigm in media studies; the domains of family home and school classroom can no longer account for the bulk of children's media exposure or experiences. Children engage with media objects, narratives, and products in school, at home, *and* in after-school care services. Their media practices are no longer isolated in one or the other environment but are increasingly mobilized across the various spaces. A third environment, OSHC, is fast becoming equally, if not more, significant than either the home or classroom.

Global changes of the late twentieth century and now, early twenty-first century, are indeed undermining core cultural concepts. The innocent child, a construction of the previous two centuries, may have outgrown even its ideological usefulness as so many cultural institutions now represent children as 'sovereign, playful, thinking consumers' (Kapur, 1999: 125). Where do we find these new sovereign children? Where do they play, and under what circumstances do they act as consumers? Does their sovereignty have boundaries? It is certain that for media consumption and production, the family home is becoming less significant as other spaces become more important to children's lives and their everyday experiences. In parallel with this geographic shift, there is currently a rise in the importance of mobile technologies and media that operate independent of fixed location. The home is no longer the exclusive place for consumption of video, television, and other media as screening technologies move towards the miniature and mobile. How will OSHC manage mobile media?

All signs suggest that OSHC populations will continue to grow as more adults work outside the home, the extended family care network vanishes, and non-supervised play is increasingly perceived as dangerous. As the terrain shifts underneath the construct of a private–public divide, gaps appear. Where the family used to be, OSHC has stepped in. It is one of the new institutions filling a gap for many children and families. But what is the nature of this space and how does it influence the development of media competency?

Looking into what children do with media and how media technologies are made meaningful through activities within particular environments is critical. What computers mean in OSHC is quite different from their meaning in the school's computer class, and yet children's understandings of media, their habits, pleasures, and preferences in use are formed across a variety of experiences gained in many different places. A child's media competency is formed 'with time' in a developmental trajectory, but it is also a cumulative process that occurs simultaneously across the different spaces and social contexts in which s/he inhabits. As children move between different spaces and regulatory schemes, they build up personal and social practices that inform their overall media use. The tendency to view media learning as a diachronic process, a process that happens over time rather than in time, relies on developmental theories of learning. Alternatively, a synchronic view of how media competency is developed makes it possible to account for the learning that occurs over time as well as that which occurs in time and in different places. In theorizing OSHC as intermediary space, I am suggesting that it contributes to a child's acquisition of media competency in a synchronic triad along with the knowledge-building activities that occur in homes and classrooms. The informal learning that goes on around play activities complements formal instruction in media use.

In the next chapter, I discuss the physical environment and community as well as external forces such as media classification and regulation that shape children's media play in OSHC. Children's multi-modal Pokemon play and strategies they have designed for turn taking at video games provide rich examples in the ethnographic tradition.

4
Pokemon on the Playground

> It's a TV show and video game and we play like we're
> the Pokemon. All my friends like playing Pokemon so
> we go on the play yard [...] and we pretend.
>
> —Thomas, 11 years old

Migratory media: Pokemon on the playground

Drawing on observations of children's media activities from several Out of School Hours Care (OSHC) services in the study, this chapter looks at how different forces shape the way media are used in play. The first part examines how certain ways of playing with media are supported by the OSHC environment. An example of Pokemon's migration from electronic screen to playground demonstrates this point. Secondly, we look more closely at how the social context and values in OSHC contour media play. This is exemplified in children's turn-taking strategies for video game play. The second half of the chapter examines official media regulation schemes operational in Australia and discusses their impact on OSHC and media play.

A few words about Pokemon provide necessary background for two of the following examples. At the time the research for this book was conducted, Pokemon trading cards were exceedingly popular. In many Australian primary schools the trading cards were banned during school hours including recess and lunchtime. Both children and OSHC staff invariably explained the ban by reciting a tale in which older children negotiated 'unfair trades' with younger children. When OSHC staff discussed the regulation with me, they often said that they did not want to spend their time soothing the tears brought about by tragic trades. One OSHC manager told me that the ban at her site was due to a Pokemon-related stabbing that allegedly occurred in an adjoining suburb. I tried to verify this report with the school principal because she was acknowledged as the local source for the story. She denied knowledge of the incident. I was, however, able to find a newspaper item from the local paper, *The Advertiser*, reporting that a 12-year-old boy in Montreal, Canada, stabbed a 14-year-old because the elder one had allegedly stolen Pokemon cards from the younger brother of the twelve year-old (29 October 1999, p. D30). The belief that such an incident occurred locally is best ascribed to urban myth and the typical moral panic that is often associated with popular children's media.

Perhaps unrelated to this report, the school principal had banned all Pokemon branded items on school grounds, including lunch boxes, folders, and clothing. If a child were to bring a Pokemon character to school, on a tee shirt, folder, or in any other form, it had to remain hidden from adult view. At the OSHC service, a child wore a tee shirt with a Pokemon character on it and she was told to cover it up with her sweatshirt. Such an extensive and strict ban was not found at any other school in the study, although many did not allow card trading during school hours. School regulation of media is usually inconsistent. Individual elements of a licensed property will fall under scrutiny and, perhaps, regulation at various times, while other brands or franchises will remain unnoticed by the regulators (adults). During my research, some schools allowed card trading while banning hand-held electronic devices such as Digimon, and others schools did just the opposite. Adult intervention and regulation is usually stimulated by highly charged incidents (like the alleged stabbing) rather than observable, general use patterns.

At five of the six sites, free-to-air (broadcast) TV is most often an option in the morning, including the service in this example. Children are allowed to watch commercial TV and do not watch the national broadcaster, ABC, even though it is popularly perceived to be the 'educational channel.' During the research period all five sites tuned into Channel 10's *Cheez TV* morning show during before-school care because it featured Pokemon cartoons at 7.30. Many children started the day at OSHC by watching the beloved Pokemon cartoon and then shifted into the time and space dimension of the classroom where the mere mention of Pokemon could land one in trouble. In the afternoon, children returned to OSHC and played 'Pokemon Stadium' on the Nintendo64 or one of the other Pokemon games on the Game Boy. When they arrived at OSHC, there was usually a Game Boy or two that had been brought from home, and occasionally a 'link cable' necessary for trading digital characters. By allowing Pokemon play, talk, trading, and celebration of all its lore, OSHC services distinguish themselves from the hosting school and classrooms and their associated regulations. Children are allowed to enjoy the current trend and most services own the Pokemon video games and Game Boy cartridges because they were, at the time, the most frequently requested by children. Pokemon is also popular with both girls and boys, so all of the sites with platforms that support Pokemon software have one or more Pokemon games. While the popularity of the Pokemon brand generated its prohibition during school hours, this same popularity secured its presence in OSHC.

The intermediary nature of OSHC also influences how children play with media at OSHC. In the following passage, 11-year-old Thomas explains how he and his friends have made Pokemon play a physical and performative game:[1]

> Thomas: It's a TV show and video game and we play like we're the Pokemon. All my friends like playing Pokemon so we go on the play yard. So we hop in the boat and we pretend that we're sailing to one of the element types in Pokemon like Ice Fighting or Flying. Then we go to that land and stick our nets in the ocean of whatever the element is, like an ocean of rocks. Then we pull out Pokemon [names several Pokemon characters]. And then you have to battle them on the ship and then catch 'em. And sometimes on the ship the captain is evil and he steals your Poke Balls (yellow tennis balls) and you have to earn them back by catching Pokemon over the side of the boat.
>
> Interviewer: Do you play characters?
>
> Thomas: We've only got the characters of Pokemon but not the characters from the [TV] show. But we've got balls, so we chuck them. You can return them and they fight. And there's this one Pokemon, Pikachu, and he doesn't like hopping.
>
> One playground area might be a shop where you buy Pokemon. One is the mating season where you have two Pokemon at the same time and you can buy Pokemon in their unevolved form. There's one [area] where you can buy Pokemon that evolve some of the time. There's the place where you can battle the King of the Island. He's a really strong Pokemon of a certain type. There's also this other playground that we sometimes go on. It's like an adventure area. We find out passwords that the Pokemon says and we go through to the games area.

Thomas is describing what I have come to call Playground Pokemon. A publicly acknowledged Pokemon expert, Thomas often gathers together a group of boys to play this chase-and-toss game around the climbing equipment on the playground. The children physically enact the actions of characters from the popular video games and recreate story lines from the morning cartoon. (Thomas does not often get to watch the programme in the morning because he is usually on the way to school at the time. His grandfather, however, tapes the show for him so he can watch it in the evenings.)

When I first observed this game, I saw a group of six boys running from climbing bars to sandpit, and from cubby house to the shipwrecked boat. When they would arrive at a new 'base,' they would hurl yellow tennis balls at one another's torsos or engage in lengthy discussions that sounded, to me, like speaking in tongues. I soon came to learn this was all about Pokemon. In this physically active and performative game, children's creative play borrows and expands on a narrative found in electronic media. The boys discussed characteristics of the different creatures, and generated 'what if' scenarios extending the games' narrative in directions that have yet to be developed by the professional writers. Patricia Palmer (1986) has suggested that this type of play is probably more common than research indicates because most research has looked at television viewing in the home and bypassed the sort of peer networks where such 'TV play' occurs (p. 148). More recent comparative studies in Europe have also found that while children at home mainly watch television alone or with family, they use television as a social lubricant among and within peer groups. David Buckingham and Julian Sefton-Green (2003) have argued that Pokemon is particularly well suited to the type of migration, transformation, and creative extension that I have described here because the text itself is portable and playing with Pokemon 'requires' activity. Placing Pokemon in the OSHC environment amplifies the features of mobility and creativity because the multiple platforms on which Pokemon exists are often in play simultaneously at OSHC, the play is most often social, and both boys and girls are involved.

Playground Pokemon illustrates how OSHC mediates between different types of play (media-centred, imaginative, physical), different media (TV, video games, collecting), and seemingly separate spaces (home, school, OSHC). At this OSHC service, the children have access to Nintendo64 with Pokemon Stadium software, Game Boys with several different Pokemon game cartridges, and children are allowed to bring these items from home to OSHC as well. Sometimes Thomas brings video games that OSHC does not have. Several of the children bring their Game Boys to OSHC and trade Pokemon characters across the link cable. The characters from the Game Boy cartridges can also be loaded onto the Nintendo64 console platform. Using the link cable to facilitate electronic trading, a child can acquire a number of Pokemon for his/her home use without parents having to purchase them. OSHC is an agora, a meeting place, and a market, for the exchange of Pokemon characters. Digitally replicated and physically transported from OSHC to homes, the traded characters end up in several Nintendo consoles.

Thomas's game of Playground Pokemon and the cross-platform trading of Pokemon characters demonstrate how children's media play is not restricted to the dimension of any particular screen, that is the space in which it is first experienced. Instead, children's media practices and competencies are often mobile, just like the personal technology of the Game Boy. Media competency resides in the body, and children's bodies are often difficult to contain, as we see when watching children perform the stories of Pokemon worlds on the playground.

When their turn at the Nintendo64 console is finished, Thomas and the other boys are able to take their pleasure in Pokemon out to the playground. The playground game draws on several different media (television, film, video games, WWW, and collecting cards), adapting Pokemon play to the given space of the playground and transforming the playground into a fictional world. The game also incorporates the existing playground equipment by designating the jungle gym as the 'incubator' in which Pokemon 'evolve,' while the boat and cubby house serve other functions of this expanding story world. While all the children acknowledge that Thomas is the inspiration behind this game, they too are capable of performing this set of transfers from media space to physical space, from media play to imaginative, physical play.

The mediation of media is always coupled with the geographic mediation between OSHC and other places where media play occurs. For Thomas, that other space is home. In an informal discussion with his mother, when I was seeking her permission for Thomas to participate in the study, she told me how pleased she is that he gets to 'play' Pokemon at OSHC because his older siblings are not interested in this craze. They tire of hearing him talk about it at home, and so his mother believes that OSHC provides a place for him to pursue his interest with people who share his passion for Pokemon. Another mother has told me that she likes OSHC because her son, an only child, gets 'access to media the he doesn't have at home and [this] allows him to be literate about these things, like Pokemon.' The literacy that she refers to is a cultural literacy and one that can be traded, like capital, at the moment. She also believes that his video game playing at OSHC will ensure that he does not pressure her to buy a video game machine for home, an expensive investment that she does not want to undertake at the moment.

Both of these mothers are aware that their sons construct their identities, to some degree, with reference to their knowledge and fluency with media and popular culture. These parents have a positive attitude towards OSHC and media use within it. For both mothers, the intermediary function of OSHC, with respect to Pokemon, is that it provides a space away from home where Pokemon can be valued and their children's interests and skills can be validated by peer recognition. OSHC is the place where children can, through media, express their '"common culture" and "facilitate learning communities,"' as Buckingham and Sefton-Green (2003) have noted of Pokemon.

The social shape of taking turns

Looking closely at the way children take turns and share video games at OSHC gives us an insight into some of the social dimensions of media play. The fundamental rule of video game play at OSHC is that everyone who wants a turn gets a turn. This is no simple task when demand is high and resources are scarce. At most services turn limits on console video games and Game Boys are maintained at ten minutes per child. This is an extremely short turn at video game play, and for games that have been designed for immersion and long play, the short turn might be frustrating to the player because not much progress can be achieved in the short time frame. The children, however, have found a way to extend their video game playing time. By pooling the ten-minute turns of four children, they form a group. The four children then share in a 40-minute 'go' for the group. I describe this system as 'synchronous turn sharing.'

The synchronous turn-sharing system has been standardized by the children at all the services but one. At this exceptional service, the Service Director prohibits children from playing video and computer games in groups. The Director thinks it is better for children to 'be active, physically active or artistic.' The rule was explained to me:

> What we don't like is a group of ten or 12 kids huddled around the Play Station. We think there are more positive things they could do with their time than standing around. It's too easy for them – nothing is asked of them to passively sit there and watch even if they're not playing.
>
> (Interview, 10 March 2003)

Children do prefer to play video and computer games in groups and playing usually incorporates a sort of spectator gallery where an audience interacts with the players, calling comments, giving instruction, cheering, and so forth (OFLC, 1999; Palmer, 1986; Suss et al., 2001; Vered, 1998a). Suss et al. (2001) have verified this fact in a European comparative study and state that

> Children and teenagers use media in the company of friends. Media usage is just one part of everyday life and interaction with other people takes place during it. Television viewing mainly takes place in family situations, whereas console or computer games are often played with friends as well.
>
> (p. 39)

As children get older and orient themselves outside the family home, they say, 'the media which are mostly used at home become less important and media which can be used in public places, or "mobile media", are more popular.'

Children's preferred style of media play, with friends and in a group, helps develop social skills and relations, and is not an example of children 'just standing around.' They are doing something; they enjoy what they are doing, even though it may be neither artistic nor athletic. Playing video games, knowing video games, and watching others play are all activities that carry a certain cultural capital. Children can use this capital when negotiating and asserting their positions in other social relationships and circumstances. Video game play, like knowledge of Pokemon lore, provides opportunities for children to use space and place, as Smith and Barker have described it, to further the continual processes of 'restructuring power and identity' (2000: 315). Through game play, children are able to practice and assert their positions as 'novice,' 'expert,' 'veteran,' and the like, relative to game culture and peer culture.

Ironically, the director who dislikes children watching video games does like having the games at the site because, he says, 'The noise and the color [of video games] adds a bit of life to the whole thing when you walk into the room and there are games going and stereos on – it's a nice atmosphere.' Indeed, the same qualities in video games that add ambience and atmosphere to the room also attract children. The regulation on video game play at this site conflicts with the appeal of these games and prohibits children from having a turn long enough to actually make progress in the game. Faced with this restriction, the children have found a way to customize play so that they can enjoy video games in their depth and complexity.

Since they are not allowed to play in groups, children at this service have not adopted the synchronous turn-sharing system. They cannot use the simultaneous, multi-player approach so common in other services because it would generate the unwanted cluster of children; group play involves too many children around the Play Station at one time. In other words, collaborative play in shared space is not allowed. To extend game play time and still conform to the adult regulation, these children have developed a way to share the game serially. Saving the game with a password before it is concluded, the player 'passes on' the game, still in play, to the next player. The password is revealed and the new player (hopefully) furthers the progress before handing the game over to another. This continues until the game is complete or abandoned. Since the game can go on like this for several days, the idea of third place is further reinforced. Some children play the game at home between OSHC sessions and practice the play, learn new moves, or discover new cheats. As a group, they may also discuss the game during school time. The video game played in OSHC exists with the children wherever they go.

The individual and serial form of play allows each child to contribute to the game and share in the play to a greater extent than would be possible if the game were abandoned after a single ten-minute session. In effect, they are playing as a group and gaining some of the benefits of group play. Rather than group play, which relies on a synchronous turn-taking system, the children have developed an asynchronous, or serial, system of turn taking that capitalizes on multi-player skill, but does so across time and turns by utilizing the password function. While children at other services collaborate spatially, these children negotiate collaboration as an aspect of time.

I have asserted that OSHC philosophically embraces child-directed leisure activities, but it is obvious that there are points when practice and ideology conflict. In the particular situation described above, the director misses a fine point by not recognizing how group play and spectatorship in electronic game play can build social relationships and skills. By restricting (simultaneous) group play, the negotiation of personal and interpersonal power relations through game play is jettisoned. The children, however, have recognized what the adult has overlooked. Their inventive serial form of group play accommodates adult perceptions of 'proper play' (that is, playing one at a time) while still achieving some of the pleasures of group play: passing into more levels, sharing in an achievement, and making a social activity of what might otherwise be an individual one. In this situation, children have demonstrated a point made by Brian Sutton-Smith in his treatise on toys and culture. Sutton-Smith noted, as early as 1986, that video games have the potential to be used solitarily, but like other toys and games, children prefer to play with other people and will do so with video games, given the opportunity. The social context of OSHC, which demands that children play together at most activities, does not come to an abrupt end at the interface of computer or video screen. The social context determines to what extent a video game will be a solitary or social experience.

By circumventing the prohibition on group play, as these children have done for themselves, they create opportunities for peer tutoring and development of new friendships as enacted in the roles of 'player' and 'spectator.' They also make video game play more like the other activities at OSHC, all of which are usually group activities. Drawing, art making, reading, and even playing with the 'personal technology' of Game Boy devices are group activities in OSHC (see Figure 4.1). It is common to see three children sharing a book or a Game Boy, and drawing and art making are almost always conducted around a table where children share the materials and the production space (see Figure 4.2). The social nature of OSHC is enjoyed and exercised by children across a variety of endeavours, including media play.

Despite the rigid restrictions on video game play, this is the only service that supports media production as an activity, outside of the somewhat limited output that children produce with computers. Their Movie Magic programme is discussed at length in Chapter 8.

Formal regulation and media classification

Pokemon on the playground and the clever ways that children manage to extend the pleasure of play under time limitations show us that they find their media play stimulating, engaging, and entertaining. Adults, however, are sometimes wary of children being so attracted to media and they worry that, unlike other types of recreation, media play is not only a waste of time but also potentially harmful. Caution against children's use of media usually turns on one of two concerns: the activity itself or the content. Either it is how children might use their access to media that is worrisome or it is the media content that raises alarm. Historically the 'social messages' of media narratives, an issue of content, have been viewed by adults as poor examples for children (Luke, 1990; Nikken and Jansz, 2006). This view is so pervasive

Figure 4.1   Children playing with Game Boy

Figure 4.2   Group play at traditional activity

that many countries, such as Australia, have state regulatory or industry bodies that assess and evaluate media content.

In Australia, the OFLC assesses film, video, and computer games for their content and assigns a classification (rating) to inform consumers. A film or game's classification is meant to signal its acceptability for audiences: G (General), PG (Parental Guidance Recommended), M (Recommended for Mature Audiences), MA 15+ (Persons under 15 years must be accompanied by an adult), R 18+ (Restricted to persons 18 years and older). The OFLC is an agency of the federal government that supports and administers the working of the Classification Board, a 20-member body that makes decisions on film, video, and computer game classification. Each film, video, or computer (video) game that is to be distributed must be classified by the Board. The distributor applies to the Board and pays a fee to gain the classification. Unlike the United States where 'ratings' for film and games are assigned by industry bodies, in Australia the task is part of broader legislation and thus enacted and enforced by an agency of government.

Among other purposes, classification is meant to protect minors from 'material likely to harm or disturb them' (The Code, www.oflc.gov.au). In addition, the OFLC is obliged to provide consumer advice about the content of films and computer games that it classifies. (For G classification, the Act gives the Board the option whether to provide consumer information.) According to the OFLC, consumer advice 'helps consumers decide what they and their family should view, read or play, by indicating what sort of content material contains.' Whether or not classification informs or assists consumers is unproven. That is to say, how much faith the public puts in the classifications (G, PG, M, and so on) and how much they rely on these codes, when making decisions about which film to see or which video to hire, is not clear. It is clear, however, that the OFLC is not always in tune with children's taste, as was the case with *Harry Potter and the Philosopher's Stone*, and many children in this study said that they regularly play M-classified games at home. This would suggest that their parents buy the games either for the children or themselves and that the children at least have access to the games even if they were not purchased on their behalf.

The six classifiable elements under the current (2005) Australian law are nudity, drug use, course language, sex, violence, and themes (referring to the narrative themes) (www.oflc.gov.au). The OFLC is charged with carrying out the Classification Act, a national law, and states and territories are responsible for enforcing it. That is to say, if an objection is raised in New South Wales, it is the New South Wales state authority that responds, not the OFLC.

Many children enjoy M-rated games, and some OSHC services allow children over ten years old to play games that are off-limits to the younger children. Offering M-rated games occurs only when there is sufficient space and hardware to support two separate game machines in separate locations. Some services are able to facilitate age segregation during school holidays when classes are not in session and more physical space, and some hardware, become available to Vacation Care services. While services are aware of the OFLC guidelines, they have shaped their own policies on a combination of factors that includes the taste culture of children 10 to 12. Some services require that children bring written permission from their parents if they expect to play M-classified games during Vacation Care. For the day-to-day fare in after-school care, games with G and PG classifications are the norm.

Australian television also carries content advice, and broadcasting legislation acknowledges that there are certain times of day when children are more likely to be viewing. In these periods extra restrictions apply to broadcast content, and broadcasters are encouraged to air programmes for children. The Australian Communication and Media Authority or ACMA (known until July 2005 as the Australian Broadcasting Authority, ABA), a federal government body, outlines qualities and characteristics for Children's (C) and Pre-School (P) programmes in the *Commercial Television Standards 2005*.

The Standards explain that

> A children's program is one which: (a) is made specifically for children or groups of children; (b) is entertaining; (c) is well produced using sufficient resources to ensure a high standard of script, cast, direction, editing, shooting, sound and other production elements; (d) enhances a child's understanding and experience; and (e) is appropriate for Australian children.
>
> (www.acma.gov.au)

Moreover, a broadcaster must air a 'combined total of at least 390 hours of C material and P material in each year' including 'at least 260 hours of C material and at least 130 hours of P material ... A licensee must broadcast C material for a continuous period of time of not less than 30 minutes: (i) every weekday between the hours of 7.00 AM and 8.00 AM or 4.00 PM and 8.30 PM; to a total of at least 130 hours per year in addition' (*Commercial Television Standards 2005*). (While these licensure requirements are more strict than those applied in the US, they are considerably less proscriptive than requirements in other countries, such as Singapore, for example, where many more hours of children's programming is required by law.)

The Commercial Television Industry Code of Practice (CTI Code) complements the *Commercial Television Standards*. The CTI Code is based on the OFLC classification guidelines but includes additional classifications of C, P, and AV (adult violence), in addition to G, PG, M, and MA 15+ (www.freetvaust.com.au). The CTI Code requires that 'an appropriate classification symbol of at least 32 television lines in height, in a readily legible typeface, must be displayed for at least 3 seconds' at the programme's start and after each break. Consumer advice is required 'about the principal elements that contribute to a program's classification, and indicates their intensity and/or frequency' for all MA and AV programmes, all PG films, and for any 'PG classified program broadcast between 7.00 PM and 8.30 PM on weekdays or between 10.00 AM and 8.30 PM on weekends that contains material of a strength or intensity which the licensee reasonably believes parents or guardians of young children may not expect.' The non-commercial, public television stations, SBS and ABC, use the OFLC guidelines to classify their own television programming while the commercial stations follow the CTI Code.

In the main, film, electronic games, and television in Australia are classified and regulated only for their content. There is minimal regulation of advertising to children and the most highly specified restrictions apply to food and beverage advertising. The CTI Code states that advertising directed to children for food and beverages must not encourage 'unhealthy eating or drinking habits' which is defined as 'excessive or compulsive consumption of food and/or beverages' or 'an inactive lifestyle' which means 'not engaging in any or much physical activity as a way of life.' In effect there is little restriction on food advertising to children in Australia, even during P and C programme broadcasts. Although the national broadcaster, ABC, offers a commercial-free alternative, the majority of the broadcast spectrum is commercial.[2]

For a range of reasons adults exercise regulatory authority over children's media access and use in ways much less formalized than the legislative regulations outlined above. Such ad hoc and often informal regulation is important to the degree that it can legitimate or undermine a view of children's media play as useful recreation. When adults do not believe that media play is a sensible way for children to spend their leisure time, it is unlikely that they will provide media hardware and content to promote productive use of these media. In a recent study of parental management of children's media use, Peter Nikken and Jeroen Jansz (2006) have confirmed that parents who believe video game play has positive effects on learning and cognition are more likely to play these games with their children and that parents restrict the media use of young children and girls more than they do for older children and boys (p. 185). Unfortunately, once restriction and prohibition are adopted as methods to manage children's media use, the other options for adult participation and engagement are foreclosed. That is to say, parents who restrict media access and use are not likely to engage in co-play with children and are less likely to engage in discussion about their children's media play.

As I have shown in earlier chapters, children's media practices are developed over time and across different spaces and communities of practice. School classrooms, computer rooms, family homes, and OSHC services, all offer children access to a variety of entertaining and educational media. Children develop their media competencies from experiences acquired in all of these places, although some of their experiences are constructed as educational and others as recreational. As an intermediary space, OSHC can offer both education and entertainment without having to justify either. The nature of media use in OSHC is, however, contoured by many factors, including formal regulation and consumer advice, school-based rules and attitudes towards media, children's play practices, and adult attitudes towards media use as a form of play. The next chapter looks at theories of play to better understand how media play is legitimated as a valuable recreational activity in OSHC.

5
The Place of Media in Children's Leisure

> The classic theories of play's function were virtually that the player did not learn anything. Play was surplus energy, relaxation, recreation or catharsis. We could argue that these theories were themselves a by-product of the work ethic. They reflected the same duality of work and play which characterized the economic life of industrial societies, an ethic in which work is valued and play is not. In these theories, therefore, play is given only a derivative or a projective status. This kind of thinking is still widely prevalent in ordinary notions of play, and in ordinary disbelief in its value.
>
> —Brian Sutton-Smith, 1979

Principles of play

Play is a social activity which, like most others, offers learning opportunities but does not in all instances guarantee learning. Sutton-Smith has described two paradigms on play. The primary one, he says, holds that 'play is an activity taken up voluntarily, usually by a solitary player, and often with objects which are under his control. As a result of his [sic] activity or fantasy with those objects, the subjects make individual gains either in cognitive or creative organisation.' The secondary paradigm, common to anthropology, folklore, and sociolinguistic disciplines, sees play as a 'way of organizing collective behavior, that it is a form of human communication and that it reflects the enculturative processes of the larger society' (1979: 1).

Among the many activities that Out of School Hours Care (OSHC) provides for children is the opportunity to practice and extend their media competency through media play. This is not a claim that all play is educational or that we can easily identify and isolate specific learning outcomes from play. Rather, the point is that individuals sometimes learn, or extend their knowledge, through recreational activity and play.

In the same way that play has been trivialized by theories that construct it as 'the opposite of work,' or what happens once the important things are done, entertainment media and leisure time dedicated to media use have also been trivialized. Play that involves entertainment media is twice as vulnerable to charges of uselessness. Given the cultural and ideological weight such views bear, legitimating media play poses quite a challenge. Identifying the points of intersection where media use and play meet, we can begin to construct a more respectable profile for media use among children's leisure-time pursuits.

Adult attitudes towards children's media use vary but, for the sake of description, let us imagine a continuum. A positive attitude towards children's media use is one that respects children's interest and enthusiasm for media play by actively supporting their activities through a variety of means. A negative attitude is one that constructs media play as an undesirable way for children to spend their leisure time. A negative attitude is sometimes revealed in the beliefs and opinions staff express about media and media play and in the low priority that is assigned to media provision and its use within the play environment. A neutral attitude, naturally, is in between the two. The provision and management of media play is neither enthusiastically supported nor ignored completely with a neutral attitude. Management might neither initiate investment in media play nor seek to quash media play when it develops 'organically.' When adults hold a neutral attitude towards children's media play, it is children themselves who must stimulate and invest in the media environment and activities. In order to support pleasurable media play, adults need to hold a positive attitude towards media and children's media play as an activity or, if holding a neutral view, to respond positively to children's initiatives and prompts. All other circumstances being equal, it is unlikely that media play will be invested in and developed well if adults, be they service management or parents, hold negative attitudes about entertainment media and children's interest in them. A negative view of media play might even undermine the media practices that children themselves develop.

Although I have argued in Chapter 2 that Australian OSHC services embrace media activities as a legitimate form of play, that embrace is a loose one. Relative to the US and UK provision of media for recreational purposes, Australian OSHC services do indeed support and promote media use as a legitimate form of play. Not all Australian OSHC services, however, provide the positive environments and attitudes that were found in the sample study of six sites. As I noted in Chapter 4, some service directors and staff workers are critical of some media practices and supportive of others.

Adult views of children's interest in entertainment media often suffer from, what Brian Sutton-Smith has identified as, a fundamental contradiction in how we value children's play more broadly. Basically, adults are undecided on whether or not play is good in itself. Sutton-Smith holds that opposing opinions on play persist:

> The desire for children to make progress in development and schooling has led to play's being considered either as a waste of time (the view of educational 'conservatives') or a form of children's work (the belief of educational 'progressives'). The one view is that play is not usefully adaptive, the other that it is.
>
> (1997: 19)

OSHC is in between the two worlds of home and classroom and two worldviews about children's lives and what counts as appropriate recreation, leisure activity, and play. The intermediary nature of OSHC places it in a unique position to provide opportunities for learning through play. On the one hand, OSHC grants children time and space to play. On the other hand, their play may be critically viewed if it is not productive, in what Sutton-Smith calls adaptive and progressive ways. Media play is especially vulnerable to criticism because it is often popularly viewed as a waste of time. The challenge for OSHC services is to provide media play opportunities that are seen to be productive.

Since play is fundamental to a child's development, play is often positioned as 'child's work.' Framing play as work puts an enormous, and unnecessary, burden on play. In such formulations, the ideological role of an adult 'work ethic' is replaced with a 'play ethic' for children. Not only must children play but they also must be productive in play. Productivity is measured as progress but it is not the type of progress that is characterized by advancing levels in a video game. The progress that adults would like to see in play is learning that can be transferred from the play context for use in other aspects of life, those that adults deem more serious. Since the outcomes of media play are not easily measured, except when levels in the video game are taken into account, it is a ready target for criticism. And yet, when you ask children where they learned to perform some function on the computer or where they learned to use a particular software programme, they often say a friend showed them how, or some other child has it at home. They are learning in recreational and social settings that are not explicitly instructional.

Children characterize their play as 'having fun, being outdoors, being with friends, choosing freely, not working, pretending, enacting, fantasy and drama, and playing games' (Sutton-Smith, 1997: 49). These are all attributes of the OSHC experience and especially applicable to media play in OSHC. Many of the children interviewed for this book used exactly the same words when describing their pleasure in media play.

Eight-year-old Kayla said that she liked to play 'Pokemon Stadium' because 'It's fun and it's really popular with other children. So when I ask them to play they always say yes because they want to play. It's really cool.' Blossom, another eight-year-old said, 'It's more fun to play with a friend because a friend can cheer you on or go "booh" 'cuz they're losing.' The free choice associated with software selection was important to ten-year-old Amelia: 'There's more of them and you get to choose more ... they have all these ones that you get to choose out of in the box. There's [sic] ones that you don't have to fight on. I don't like fighting games that much.' Bill also praised the variety and range of computer games at OSHC: 'At my house I only have one game; here they have about 150 games.' Video game play, the newest of entertainment media in OSHC, is the most controversial. Adults worry that children spend too much time in front of the screen without demonstrating physical or creative exertion. Children, on the other hand, attribute to video game play the qualities that are fundamental to play itself. Children experience video games as play.

Recognizing the value of group or cooperative play is also important and particularly useful in understanding the value of media play at OSHC because media play is usually pursued as a group activity. Sutton-Smith (1997) has said of group play that it

> provides participants with solidarity, identity, and pleasure. The constant modern tendency to think of play as simply a function of some other more important cultural process (psychological or sociological) tends to underestimate the autonomy of such play cultures. It makes it difficult to understand that the major obvious function of play is the enjoyment of playing or being playful within a specific culture of play. The most important identity for players is typically the role that they are playing (first baseman, 'it,' trickster). Whatever else might be subserved by that identity is generally a secondary matter during the moments of play.
>
> (p. 106)

Children's media play at OSHC is by necessity most often a group endeavour. Limited media resources, a democratic imperative, and the obligation to be inclusive across the wide age and taste range of children ages 5 to 12 ensures that children rarely have the chance to play with media alone at OSHC. The most prominent examples of group-play cultures have developed around video game play. These play cultures vary from service to service because media provision, positioning, and adult attitudes towards media are not uniform.

What is deemed productive play and what qualifies as a useful leisure-time pursuit are inconsistent among OSHC services, and the values that adults ascribe to children's activities are often relative. This is particularly poignant in the latest assault on media play. For the past few years in Australia as elsewhere, there has been growing concern around the issue of childhood obesity. In discussion, debate, and speculation on the causes of rising childhood obesity, media use is frequently singled out as a cause. Media play, it is said, is a sedentary activity, and the amount of time children spend playing video games and watching TV is time away from healthier activities, presumably those that require physical activity. Such displacement theories are even endorsed by health insurance providers and have recently appeared central to many articles on children's health and fitness. For example, in the April 2003 members' newsletter *wellplan*, issued by Australian private health insurance provider, Australian Unity, ten 'practical steps to fitness' are recommended for children's health and fitness. The very first among them is to 'turn off the TV, or at least limit the number of hours per day your children sit watching TV or playing computer games' (p. 5). A similar news item appeared in *feelbetter*, the newsletter of another insurance company in Autumn 2002. Entitled 'Chubbier than Ever,' the item began, 'Days spent slumped in front of computer games, or the television, are making our kids fat.' The article reduces the complex issue of obesity in advanced capitalist societies to 'simple lack of physical activity,' which is characterized by TV viewing and computer game play. The reader is meant to conjure an image of a fat child watching TV or playing video games and not the image of a fat child drawing or reading. While video game play and television use are nominated as a-physical activities, other sedentary activities are ignored. Reading and drawing are never mentioned in these articles on 'fat kids' but it is electronic entertainment and children's media play that are assigned responsibility (see Figures 2.2 and 7.1). The fear that media play is replacing physical play is based on anecdotal observation of children at home, where children are most likely to use media alone and in isolation.

Vickii Jenvey has recently reviewed the research on children, media and obesity and concludes that, the evidence does not 'support the proposal that television viewing displaces time available for more vigorous activity' because

> results from research investigating an association between television and other passive media consumption and early onset of obesity in young children have been equivocal, and underlying mechanisms proposed to lead to obesity have not been delineated clearly by researchers. Potential methodological shortfalls in existing literature ... included failure of some studies to collect data on all children's leisure time activities; existing nutritional practices in the family context, especially types of foods provided by parents; parents' own level of physical activity and eating habits and food preferences modeled by parents of young children.
>
> (2007: 817)

A responsible and thorough explanation for the rise in childhood obesity must address changes in diet, sleep, and rest patterns; consumption of prepared and packaged foods which contain high levels of fats, salts, and sugars; and changes in overall lifestyle and activity levels, hereditary propensities, among other factors. While television viewing and electronic game play may substitute for some activities, they do not substitute for all childhood activity. Moreover, video game play and television viewing are often more physically performative for children than are other activities which are not blamed for conserving calories. In a 2004 study of children's views about their physical activity and health, researchers noted with some surprise that

> Children did not consider TV and computer games as barriers to physical activity. They see them as consistently coexisting and often promoting activity. [...] They described a world in which homework, TV, the computer, sport and play could and should coexist. [...] Many were moved to try physical activity after seeing options on TV. Others said they could only watch TV for so long (often when bored) before wanting to play.
>
> (MacDougall, Schiller, and Darbyshire, p. 383)

These remarks are derived from the evaluation of focus group discussions that were part of a larger study of 204 Australian children. Researchers are subsequently looking at ways to use television as a motivational tool to increase children's physical activity.

Reading, although generally a sedentary activity and one that is normally less physically demanding than video game play, is almost unanimously viewed as a productive leisure-time activity for children and adults alike. Drawing and art making are also viewed as worthwhile activities for children, despite their sedentary nature (and in the case of craft making, its history as child labour as I have explained in Chapter 2). Reading for pleasure and making art are among the 'adaptive and progressive' activities that are usefully productive, while watching television and playing video games are activities for which measuring productivity is difficult.

At OSHC, as I have argued and will elaborate further in Chapter 6, children's media play is often combined with physical activity and even their television-viewing practices are often quite physical and athletic. Moreover, the amount of time they spend on media play at OSHC is considerably less than the time spent in media use at home. Overall, the time spent with media and the nature of that activity at OSHC is far more active, social, and time limited than in family homes.

Measuring the benefits of play

The benefits of media play, especially with entertainment media, are not always directly related to curriculum and are not immediately applicable to the schooling-career path. Whether or not specific types of media play are adaptive and progressive cannot be easily measured. The productive outcomes of media play are not easily identifiable, quantifiable, nor guaranteed. Several studies, however, have shown that children who are keen video game players are often interested in and skilled with computers, and group-play around media, like any other group-play, requires skills in social negotiation. Recent research on children's physical activity has also identified ways in which television and other media stimulate physical activity. These studies are now confirming what television scholars have known for a long time, people 'watch' television while doing a range of other things; for children, these activities often include dancing, jumping, wrestling, and other physical play.

Participation in group-play cultures at OSHC, whether constituted around media play or other activities, is valuable in the ways that Sutton-Smith has identified: helping to foster membership, identity, and giving pleasure. In particular, because skill acquisition can be reflected in game play performance, video game play also offers opportunities for children to acquire cultural and social capital within the play culture and wider OSHC community. Glynda Hull and James G. Greeno have described after-school programmes as offering 'an especially powerful alternative learning site where children who haven't been successful in school can nonetheless develop agentive identities in relation to new literacies' (2006: 91). This is evident in OSHC when some children become known as experts at certain video games similar to the way in which other children are recognized for their athletic or artistic skills. Such peer recognition can serve as social lubricant and assist a child in gaining access to a wider social circle or to enter into social exchanges with greater ease.

Although they are difficult to pinpoint and measure, the social benefits of media use and media play have been reported for many years. In 1986 Patricia Palmer noted that children played with one another,

> around the set as they viewed and even incorporating material from on screen into their talk and actions ... children use TV content to initiate social events, making comments to and demands upon those around them, including parents, based on the commercials they were watching at the time.
>
> (1986: 145)

Reviewing the findings of her home study of children watching the Australian programme *Play School* alongside the findings from earlier studies, Palmer says that children's television viewing is social in at least two ways. Firstly, children's interaction with television is 'part of their everyday social behaviour.' Secondly, 'television viewing was often part of the ongoing social relationships within families.' More important for its implications relative to the peer-group setting of OSHC, Palmer says that 'it is likely that play using TV is common between friends, but the location of the observation at home limited its occurrence' in her study (p. 148). Palmer, like so many others, studied children's home viewing of television and, thus, could not report on peer-group play although she strongly suspected that television would be incorporated into children's group-play. Playground Pokemon, as described in the previous chapter, is a quintessential example of how TV and video games can stimulate and provide a base for physical play that is also rich in narrative creativity.

Palmer concludes that the adult view of children's television watching as 'zombie-like' is based on a 'prejudice against television' that has produced an imaginative, rather than documented, characterization of TV viewing. When Palmer wrote this article in 1986, video games were not as popular or widely available as they are now. The worrisome medium that held children's attention and the gaze of researchers was television. The appeal that Palmer and others have noted for television now also applies to video games and other media. As she says, 'If it were not associated with television but with classroom teaching, children's "intent viewing" would probably be rewarded with praise' (p. 150). I have argued the same point for leisure-time pursuits in an effort to demonstrate that not all play is equally valued by adults. Art making and reading for pleasure are pursuits that adults approve of, while media play is often viewed as a poor alternative to those more traditional and more prestigious activities.

So why are we so suspicious of media and children's media play? Why is it that adults find it difficult to legitimate media play as valuable play? In addition to displaying the cultural confusion that informs our understandings of play, media play, whether it is video game play, computer use, or watching a DVD, also bears the burden of a legacy of unease with electronic and communication media more generally.

Television, being the most widely studied of the media that we find in OSHC, provides an important historical context for understanding the present-day ambiguity around children, media, and play. Anxieties about television's place and value in life have been reported since the earliest studies of the medium and the same arguments are repeated with each new medium to the market, including video games and mobile phones most recently. In the British Mass Observation studies of the 1940s, as television was just entering British homes, the hallmark substitution or displacement theory is expressed clearly when adults talk about TV:

> There are so many things I can do in my leisure time while listening to and enjoying the wireless, for example, reading, carving and modelling. I am so afraid that television would prove so attractive that my spare time would be spent straining my eyes looking into a distant screen.
>
> (Mullan, 1997: 22–3)

People were afraid that watching television would take over their leisure time and substitute for or displace other activities.

The displacement theory also applied in the US context as Lynn Spigel (1992) demonstrates in her account of the elaborate processes by which the family home and family time shifted to accommodate television. Bob Mullan (1997) relays a story from the Mass Observation studies about a woman who was concerned that the quality of meals she served to her husband would be diminished if her attention were distracted from cooking and focussed instead on the television.

In *Make Room for TV*, Spigel includes an advertisement for the TV-oven (1992: 74). With a TV-oven installed in her kitchen, the cook (woman of the house) could easily prepare a meal *and* watch television at the same time (presumably a cooking show would be a wise selection). Those responsible for marketing television understood how strong the belief was in the displacement theory and sought to allay fears of television's all-consuming distraction with campaigns for the 'family circle of viewing' and illustrations of television's 'natural' fit within the established arrangement of the home. Making television blend in and go 'unnoticed' was as important to marketing strategies as demonstrating its unique benefits and centrality to family leisure. Today we find the displacement theory at the heart of claims that increased media play is causing childhood obesity.

In the 1940s the expectation that television would insulate people and keep them from a wider social life was a common feature of the fear and anxiety that people had about television's introduction to the home. Such characterizations of television still circulate, but importantly, they are dependent upon the construction of television as a domestic and private medium. The fear that television makes people more private is only plausible when television is constructed as a domestic, rather than public, medium. Even this theory is flawed when we acknowledge the 'water cooler phenomenon': that people watch television at home but then talk about it with their workmates and friends in other contexts. Television often provides adults with conversation openers. The study of media use in OSHC poses challenges to the received wisdom of media scholarship by demonstrating a set of differences between domestic media use and public media use.

OSHC is a public setting and one in which all forms of media use operate quite differently from the family home, as I have shown in previous chapters. A lack of research on media use in public spaces sustains the inaccurate generalizations about media use and generates new misconceptions. Despite some useful contribution, Mullan's work perpetuates the concern about the place of media in the leisure life of children and adults with remarks like this one:

> It is perhaps true to suggest that the modern parent, juggling with jobs, time, 'family life', other people's opinions and social expectations, finds it somewhat hard to imagine what parents did with children' before television came along to absorb three or four hours of their child's day. What has been erased from collective memory is the array of daily preoccupations, like talking and playing and working

together, and being alone, that constituted family life before the advent of television.

(1997: 165–6)

While Mullan is somewhat forgiving of television, his condemnation of video games is unequivocal. 'Unlike television which helps create a common culture ... video games are profoundly individualist' (p. 164). Mullan asserts this strongly but does not offer any evidence to support his claim. This study of children's media use in OSHC shows that, to the contrary, children engage in a range of 'daily preoccupations,' including talking, playing, and working together while playing with media. Rather than substituting for traditional play activities, electronic media can complement and often extend other play activities.

Another reason that adults view media play as a poor choice for play is the legacy of the 'effects school' of research on children and media which continues, despite appropriate criticism of its methods and intent, to hold sway in many public arenas, including media regulation. The usually stated reason for media regulation like classification and consumer advice is to ensure that media do not harm viewers, especially children. Persistence of the idea that media can harm individuals is reliant upon the logics of the effects school with reference to its three main claims:

(1) media have effects on people;
(2) alleged effects are argued to be significant *and* direct;
(3) alleged effects are measurable and quantifiable.

In essence, media effects research is behaviourist, and the rise of behaviorism to paradigmatic status coincided with the widespread adoption of television in family homes, both in the US and UK. Television first aired in Australia in 1956, by which time behaviourism was the dominant paradigm of psychology and had begun to influence other disciplines as well. The evidence for direct effects is, however, quite troubled and, as David Gauntlett maintains in his thorough critique of the 'effects school,' 'the connections between people's consumption of the mass media and their subsequent behaviour have remained persistently elusive' (Gauntlett, 1998).

Unfortunately for science, parenting, and childcare, journalism's reliance on controversy coupled with research-funding preferences for quantitative studies has kept the media effects school on the front pages and foremost in the minds of the public. This study of children's media use in OSHC, to the contrary, has looked at what children do with media and how they deploy media in their play rather than asking what media does to children because it is impossible to isolate 'effects' with any assurance. Gauntlett notes that while 'a certain proportion of the public feel that the media may cause other people to engage in antisocial behaviour, almost no-one ever says that they have been affected in that way themselves.' In this study, some children objected to restrictions on M-classified games but were quick to add that they understood these rules were in place for the benefit of other, usually younger, children, but not themselves.

Beyond identifying a bias in research funding for quantitative research, Gauntlett's arguments, while thoroughly convincing, do not explain how the effects school maintains its sway when there is a wealth of research literature that contradicts the claims and findings of much effects research. Why is it that parents still believe television and video games are bad for their children and yet hope that they become 'computer literate'?

In the fundamental work, *Constructing the Child Viewer* (1990), Carmen Luke examines the history of discourse on children and television to demonstrate how the child viewer has been constructed, constrained, defined, and delimited by trends in research and their dissemination in both academic and popular press. Luke argues that the disciplines of sociology, psychology, and education primarily viewed media as a social information source for children in the early years of research (1917–53) (p. 31). That is, movies and television were information sources from which children were socialized, or learned social lessons. At the same time, research in these disciplines viewed the child and child development as measurable. Experimental studies rather than observational studies were the preferred method of inquiry because they yielded measurements, and child development could be quantified in experimental studies. Qualitative studies, like this one, do not attempt to measure outcomes but instead seek to describe the quality of experience, in this case with respect to children's leisure-time experiences with media. Luke says that media research with children has looked primarily at children's learning and that most studies, prior to the 1980s, were conducted in schools because this is where researchers had ready access to children.

On the eve of the TV era, the educational discourse had attributed to children a new dimension. By the late 1940s children and adolescents had been transformed into consumers of mass culture and mass media. For social critics, academics, and the public, the problem with children's access to and relationship with popular culture and mass media was their susceptibility to the messages of a cultural text directed at mass society, not necessarily or solely directed at children ... In the absence of an established discourse on the child and mass media, research initially proceeded on the basis of a comprehensive body of scholarship on the child as educational object.

(pp. 57–8)

Indeed, my first research project on children and media was conducted in a public school and initially sought to examine formal learning. During the early observations, I found that the informal and recreational activities around media at recess were far more interesting and so I shifted the focus of the study (Vered, 1998a, 1998b). My fascination with children's media play is likely a product of scarcity: there simply is not as much information available on children's media play as there is on children's media education.

In the early studies of TV, the 'impact' was said to be located in the mind of the child, as argued in cognitive theory, but this alleged impact was measured in and as behaviour – registered in the body (Luke, p. 17). The emphasis on education in the children's media research field must also be analysed in light of views on play and their relationship to education. As reflected in the quote opening this chapter from Brian Sutton-Smith, the dismissal of media play as trivial is an outcome of privileging education as 'not play' (1979: 314). When research shows a relationship between media use and education, children's entertainment media are taken more seriously.

Local regulation or the rules in OSHC

Although questions about the social consequences of video game violence do hold some currency in Australia, they have not been an important concern for OSHC services. As guidelines for video game selection, OSHC management normally follow the recommendations of the OFLC. While I do not always agree with the OFLC's decisions, their authority is a convenient one for OSHC services to appeal to in seeking advice. Among the services in this study, all but one restricted video games to those classified G and G8+ (now PG) during after-school care. At OSHC, the question of violence in video games is dealt with by excluding any games that would raise objection by parents. OSHC services effectively keep these debates beyond their doorstep by following the guidance provided by the OFLC.

Despite the fact that children do not have access to violent video games in after-school care, interactive games as a category of media suffer from the negative press that circulates about violent games. When the subject of violence in games was raised on the CHI-KIDS listserv in early 2004, contributor Jeffrey Kessler reported that for the week of January 24th among the top ten selling PC games six (maybe seven) were non-violent. For PlayStation2, that week, half of the top ten sellers were non-violent games, predominantly from the genre of sports simulation (CHI-Kids Listserv, 24 February 2004). Some observers have argued that video games are becoming less violent because the maturity of the market and new technologies are driving the development of more complex games to satisfy the demand for market diversification. This is indeed true for the latest gaming platforms, such as Xbox, for which many games use increasingly sophisticated 3D animation and graphic styles that generate more realistic characters and provide different game play and aesthetic features. The FIFA 2004 (soccer), Australian Rules Football ('AFL Live'), NHL (hockey), basketball, golf, and boxing games are very popular with boys in Australia. Although it can be argued that such sports are violent, this has not been an issue in the public discourse on games and violence nor on sport in general in Australia. Most parents, I would argue, believe that these games are preferable to first-person shooters (fps).

Concerns over video games in the place of children's leisure-time revisits some of the anxiety that marked the introduction of television and has plagued television ever since. Video games and unrestricted access to the Internet are the issues most frequently raised in the press today, while television is deemed to be less of a blight on the expanding media landscape. The case of children and computers is an interesting one because the computer on its own is not a concern so much as the access it provides to the Internet. Computers, it seems, are easily associated with the practise of school lessons that adults like to see children performing. Children can use computers to compose writing exercises and to practise skills with 'educational' games. Adults like to see children using computers, and infrequently question what it is children are doing with computers.

Conflicting and self-contradictory views on media play are not exclusive to OSHC but reflect a broader cultural ambivalence about play and misunderstandings about the relationships people have with media. Controversy over whether or not media play is a legitimate recreational activity for children persists in the press and among the general public. In the intermediary space of OSHC, adults and children must negotiate the cultures of school and home to reach a balance in recreation and leisure activities that appeal to children and appease parents. Adult attitudes towards media play are demonstrated most clearly in the utilization of scarce resources and how television, video playback, and video game delivery are managed. These issues are addressed in Chapters 6 and 7.

OSHC staff, who operate the services included in this study did not express concern over the level of violence or any other content issues with respect to any of the media provided in their services. For free-to-air television, mainly programmes recognized by the various regulatory authorities as 'children's programs' were screened, although this did not exclude commercial television. Video and DVD playback selections were restricted to G and PG classified materials. Video game selection also heeded the OFLC guidelines, and only in school holiday periods, during Vacation Care sessions, did some services provide an option for older children to play higher-rated games in a separate space, given their parents approved. Where stand-alone computer games were used, they were most often part of the school's collection and thus not only sanctioned for children's use but tacitly encouraged. In all of these cases, staff had a set of standards to which they could readily appeal for guidance in selection of material that would not offend. This is not to say that the materials were all 'educational' but they were certainly acceptable recreation fare. Having recourse to a set of clearly defined standards provided by the OFLC removed a certain burden from staff in that they did not have to pre-screen and calculate the appropriateness of each property before entering it into circulation. Staff were confident that the media they provided in services would meet with parental approval and not cause alarm or concern. Management of content provision was thus streamlined for staff.

OSHC staff were, however, wary of Internet access and unsure how to monitor children's free wanderings on the web. Only two of the services provided children with Internet access, one of which was provided through the school's computer facility. During the course of research, the school adopted a filtering and blocking system which meant that OSHC staff no longer had to monitor Internet access as diligently as before, but it also caused some difficulties for the children in the beginning. (This point is addressed in detail in Chapter 7.) At the other service with Internet access children were expected to be self-monitoring and staff would periodically step into the computer area to see what they were up to. During the observation period we did not encounter any conflicts, and the children did tell us that they knew the rules and were aware of the consequence for violating the rules: a ban from using the computers.

OSHC staff were satisfied with the media provisions in their services and the amount of time children dedicated to media play at OSHC. A minority of staff expressed a concern for the total amount of media play that children undertake when home use is accounted for. They implied that parents were less likely to regulate children's time in media play than OSHC services were. The more mature staff members, but not the young adults, did express uncertainty about the value of media play as recreation. Their comments can be characterized as ambivalent rather than negative. Some staff views echoed the more conservative leanings we encounter in public opinion that perhaps media play was not as valuable for children as other, more traditional, types of recreation (running on the yard, board games, art making, and cooking for instance). That is to say, they were concerned about whether or not media play was productive play. These views were presented to me in a questioning tone and staff seemed to be seeking my advice on whether or not their concern was a legitimate one. The staff members who were unsure of the value of media play were also those who claimed to know little about the newer media such as computers and video games. They generally avoided these media and chose to participate in other activities instead, leaving the media monitoring to other staff, those more comfortable with media. Such self-selection by OSHC staff supports and confirms what other studies have found for parents. Parents who know little about media are often reluctant to advise their children on media use and are sometimes more critical of media in general (Holloway and Valentine, 2001a, 2001b). In a rather simple case of fearing the unknown, adults who suspect that there is something to be concerned about, and yet do not know precisely what that might be, sometimes restrict children's access to media rather than assist them in managing its use because they do not know how to assist children.

Unlike parents, OSHC staff have the advantage of knowing what children do with media in OSHC and how they play in group settings. The ambivalence that staff expressed to me seems to be more the result of having to balance what they hear about media in popular discourse with what they observe on a daily basis. While popular discourse suggests that children and media is a dangerous mix, everyday experience in the OSHC environment demonstrates just the opposite. The most significant conflicts we observed over media use in OSHC were between children and their parents. When parents would arrive to collect their children and try to extricate them from a turn at the video game, children would occasionally become ornery. On several occasions this conflict was resolved with parents offering to hire the game for home use on the weekend or offering some sort of immediate substitute, like promising to buy the child an ice cream if the child hurried along without a fuss. Conflicts between children are so rare that none were noted in the observations.

Each of the services involved in this study operated with a neutral or positive attitude towards children's media play and most were actively seeking ways to expand media provision because it was so popular with children. The next two chapters look at the specific ways in which television, video playback, interactive games, and the Internet are managed in OSHC by staff and by children.

6
TV and Video in OSHC

> I sometimes do play outside *and* watch TV *and* play Super Nintendo *and* go on the Internet on the computer. I mean, life doesn't always revolve around playing [video] games.
>
> —Mario, nine years old, 20 September 2000

> If people bring along videos, we'll we watch them instead of cartoons or instead of Nintendo64. Instead of Nintendo64 I don't like it. If it's Pokemon [video], I really like it. 'Pokemon Stadium' starts to get a little boring, and I don't like listening to 'Pokemon Stadium.' That's why I like watching Pokemon [video] instead of Nintendo.
>
> —Bill, nine years old, 28 July 2000

This chapter examines how television and video playback are positioned in Out of School Hours Care (OSHC) services. Positioning, here, implies both the physical and social senses of the term. Even though all of the services we visited had basically the same media (TV, video, video games, and some sort of computer access), the children's play habits around media were very different from place to place. When talking about our television use, we usually say that we 'watch TV' and when we talk about video game use, we call it 'playing video games.' The way we speak about these activities tends to simplify very complex activities and relationships with and through media. There are a lot of ways to watch television and to play video games, and children in OSHC demonstrate a wide range of media practices.

There are several factors that influence and shape the way media are used in particular contexts, and each OSHC service is a unique environment with particular habits of community. Hardware and software specifications vary, the arrangement and use of physical space and media placement within that space vary, and each service regulates media use in different ways. Consequently, accessibility and usability are different from service to service, and children establish specific play and use patterns within these configurations.

Effectively, each OSHC service constitutes a community of practice around media. The physical space, budget, and social atmosphere of these places, and the intermediary nature of OSHC space, influence how media are positioned relative to other play activities, and to media practices elsewhere. The ways in which children engage with media and with one another around media at OSHC are shaped by complex circumstances. Their practices highlight the porous nature of the boundary between entertainment and education and demonstrate how contouring the environment can effect play and play behaviour.

While the focus here is on media play, it is important to remember that media play is but one option among many that OSHC offers to children. In addition to the outdoor play spaces, art and craft provisions, cooking, table tennis, billiards, foosball, guided and/or facilitated activities, and free play, all six of the services have free-to-air television, video playback, CD players, computers, and video game machines. Some also provide Game Boy devices and their cartridges.

The opening remarks to this chapter are excerpted from interviews with children. Bill began his interview by expressing how fond he is of Nintendo play and hoped the interview would not take too long because he didn't want to miss his turn at the video games. In his choice of pseudonym (Mario, of video game fame) and his comments, the first child quoted makes clear that his after-school-hours activities were quite varied and not solely dedicated to 'playing [video] games.' Once Bill was assured that he would not miss his turn at Nintendo, he explained his hierarchy of preferences and his remarks indicate the delicate balance that revolves around the television set, the screening device that is central to several forms of media.

TV monitors and media access

Despite the fact that TV may now be considered 'old media,' the television provides the most important screen in OSHC. The television set is essential to the delivery of video games, video playback, and broadcast TV programming (free-to-air). With only one television set, video playback, video games, and free-to-air television must be screened in alternation.

For instance, a service with one set might offer video game play from 3.30 p.m. to 4.30 p.m., then screen a movie from videotape or DVD from 4.30 p.m. to 5.30 p.m., and conclude the last hour of the day with free-to-air television. Scarcity of hardware resources, like having only one TV set, drives the scheduling and alternation of media use and it has proven to be an effective system for managing media access. Alternation of video playback, video game play, and TV is the method preferred by most services. The most common pattern of media scheduling is to offer broadcast television only in the late afternoon, and the children think this is an acceptable practice.

TV time and space

In Adelaide, South Australia, five free-to-air broadcast television channels were received at the time the study was conducted. Less than 30 per cent of Australian households were pay TV subscribers, and none of the OSHC services had cable or satellite. Three of the five free-to-air channels were commercial stations. The ABC and SBS channels are government subsidized and SBS now complements this funding with commercial breaks. ABC has no commercial advertising. SBS carries very little children's programming, so effectively, services choose among the other four stations. During the research phase of this project, the broadcast television schedule from 3.00 p.m. to 5.00 p.m. was dominated by soap operas and programmes for preschool children. These programmes were not particularly appealing to the OSHC age group (5–12), so services did not offer free-to-air television until late in the day, when some more interesting shows were on. In the early part of the afternoon, all the services used the television monitor to support video playback of movies or video game play.

Although the television set plays a pivotal role in access to video games and video screenings, broadcast television is not a prominent feature of the afternoon sessions. Many children commented that they rarely saw television at OSHC because they were usually gone before television came on in the late afternoon. Overall, only 46 per cent of children said they watched TV at OSHC and this figure may be inflated by the number of children who identified videotapes as what they watched on TV at OSHC. Most of the children said they watched television at OSHC when they were tired, when their friends were not there, or if one of the programmes was a favourite. One child bitterly remarked,

I watch TV every single day because my mum's always late, because of meetings. I watch the cartoons at five o'clock. *Rocko's Modern Life* is my favourite show. And it's after *Nintendo64*. There's also *Rug Rats* and *Angry Beavers*.

(Bill, 9 years old)

Only a few suggested that the addition of another TV would be an improvement to the service.

The limited access to broadcast television in OSHC is important in light of the contribution television makes to the overall balance of media in a child's life. As Maire Messenger-Davies (2001) has pointed out, it is important to ask how television fits into children's lives and how it is situated among the other demands on our time. Despite her interest in this question, Messenger-Davies's work, like most others, ignores OSHC as a site where television and other media are part of the social landscape. Certainly the balance of television, or any other medium, in a child's life needs to be accounted for across the different spaces in which a child encounters television. It may be some relief for many parents to know that broadcast television is not a very significant feature of OSHC.

Four of the six services regularly tuned the television to the ABC between 5.00 p.m. and 5.30 p.m. for about an hour. Although ABC is the national, commercial-free station, this had little to do with the channel selection. During the research phase of this study, the only station to air 'children's programming' at 5.00 p.m. was the ABC. The other stations aired game shows, news, and 'M*A*S*H' re-runs at 5.00 p.m. The offerings on the ABC were appealing to a wide range of children across the age group. Rather than a bias against commercial television, the critical factor in selecting ABC was the appeal of their programming during this time slot. The OSHC schedule and ABC's programming schedule were 'in sync.'

In the mornings, when the ABC runs programmes for preschool children, all OSHC services (before-school care) tuned to a commercial station, Channel 10, which, for the last several years has run a programme called *Cheez TV* from 7.30 a.m. to 9.00 a.m. The programme airs a potpourri of popular cartoons and is hosted by a couple of young adults who mix chat with viewer mail between the cartoons. The then popular, *Pokemon* and *Dragonball Z* cartoons were featured in the morning and anchored a variety of other media play that the children pursued at recess, lunch, and after school, including video game play and card collecting. As this book is being written, *Cheez TV* now features *SpongeBob SquarePants*, another favourite among school-aged children.

In addition to the four services that regularly tuned to ABC in the late afternoon, one service preferred a commercial station at this time, and the children liked watching *Wheel of Fortune* and *The Price is Right*. Thinking about this apparent anomaly, some features are significant. This was the smallest service in our study; they normally have fewer than 20 children in an afternoon. It operates in a working class community, adjacent to areas of high unemployment. The service itself was also experiencing economic difficulties at the time, due to the low daily attendance. While it is possible that the lower socio-economic status of the community contributes to the shape of a 'collective taste culture' that might explain the preference for (adult) game shows over children's programming, I believe that factors more local to the OSHC community are responsible. Since the service is small, staffing requirements were low and, in turn, staff knew all the children well. Staff here took on participatory roles in most of the children's activities, rather than monitoring them from a distance. Unlike the services that tuned-in to children's programming on ABC, staff at this service often watched the game shows with the children and both adults and children played along with the studio contestants. This was the only service where co-viewing was observed and it was the norm here.

The sixth service did not use television as part of their daily programming but did occasionally put on the TV in the late afternoon. The difference here is that the children could not count on or anticipate television because it was not routinely available. Broadcast television programming had a 'special' status here because it was so rarely available. Among the five services that regularly offered broadcast television in the latter part of the afternoon, a movie in progress would delay broadcast television. If a movie was still in play and a significant number of children were watching it, television would get a miss. The services with more than one TV monitor always paired free-to-air television with video playback, never with video games. In this way, one TV monitor was used as a designated game display and allowed video game play throughout the afternoon without disruption. The second monitor facilitated free-to-air TV and video playback. None of the services had three TV sets, so when a choice had to be made about which medium to abandon and which to maintain, broadcast television was always dismissed in favour of video playback or video game play.

Staff invariably said that television was put on late in the day for several pragmatic reasons. The most commonly cited reason was to draw the children inside for a late snack. Bringing the children in from the playground reduces supervision needs across multiple physical spaces and allows staff to begin their tidy-up routine for the close of the day. After hours of outdoor, physical play, many of the children were ready for another snack and this 'TV time' often facilitated the adult and child needs well. Staff also believed that television at this time of day conveniently helped to wind-down the children before they went home. Having the children inside at this time also makes it easier for parents to locate their children when they arrived to collect them. Several services offered a substantial late snack at this time and many children would come in from the playground for hot noodles or a sandwich before going home. Television time coincided with other rhythms of the day.

The services that have more than one television monitor can and often do have a range of media in use at the same time. But, having more than one TV set requires budgetary and spatial resources that simply do not exist in all services. Where there is more than one TV set, they are usually in different rooms or separated within a large common space by mobile room dividers or an arrangement of furniture that creates distinct social spaces. Soft furnishings such as bean bag chairs, cushions, and sofas can be arranged in corners to create semi-circular viewing or playing spaces in which a number of children can sit comfortably to watch a movie, television, or play a video game.

TV screens and stories

The children's views on television at OSHC were not particularly rich or complex. They had very little to say about television at OSHC, except that 'You can change the channel and stuff at home, but at after school hours care you aren't allowed to.' More interesting is the variety of ways in which children responded to the questions about television. They did not always distinguish among the media in the same terms as the research questions implied. When asked what they watched on TV at OSHC, some children answered by listing video game titles and others referred to movie titles that they had seen on video. A few children made the sophisticated distinction between watching a scheduled broadcast and watching a taped programme, such as an episode of *The Simpsons* that had been recorded the night before. Several of the services recorded *The Simpsons* and, the popular morning show, *Cheez TV* to play in the afternoons. Several children struggled over whether this counted as 'watching television' or 'watching a video.' A similar difficulty was faced when I asked them about video game play.

In the early stages of the research, I realized an oversight in the questionnaire design. Not recognizing the social importance of Game Boy to children's media culture, I did not include a question about this mobile medium on the questionnaire. It was not until several children had volunteered Game Boy, as part of their response to the question about video games at OSHC, that I realized my omission. When I asked if they ever played video games at OSHC, several children answered yes, and then elaborated with comments about Game Boy play, to my surprise. I had overlooked Game Boy for two inter-related reasons. First, I had not thought of Game Boy as a 'video game' because I based my distinction on the delivery platform. I thought of Game Boy as a personal rather than social technology. I was thinking about technology and hardware rather than narrative and software in the first instance. Since I defined video games as console games, in opposition to computer games, I did not anticipate the importance of Game Boy devices. I was very surprised to find Game Boys in OSHC because they are small and mobile, easily lost, misplaced, or damaged. While not all the children included Game Boy in their thoughts on video games, it was mentioned often enough and sometimes with critical acumen that I revised the interview template to include questions specifically about Game Boy (see Appendix 2). Several older and experienced video game players made a point to distinguish Game Boy games from other platforms because Game Boy graphics were only two dimensional and some commented on the lack of colour in Game Boy.

The range and variation that the children expressed in their responses, to what I thought were quite media-specific questions, suggested that my understanding of media was somewhat different to theirs. Children often discussed media in terms that reflected their experiences rather than the marketing objectives of the companies that produce and sell media. Since video games are screened on the TV monitor and many children watched while others played, some children talked about this experience as 'watching TV.' They would say that sometimes they watched 'Diddy Kong Racing' or other video games, in the same way that one would name a television programme. Rather than an expression of naïveté, such remarks suggest that children do not necessarily distinguish media in the terms common to technical and industrial practices. Rather, it is the narrative content and the social experience of media play that are sometimes most important to children's practices, and consequently their interpretations reflect the significance of these practices and the values that children themselves ascribe to them.[1] The different ways that children distinguish television, video, and video games should not suggest that they do not make distinctions among the media. Rather, it points to the importance of inter-media relations in children's media practices, the fluid movement of narrative content across platforms and places.

In Chapter 4, I discussed how a group of children played an out-door chase and tag game based on Pokemon, the penultimate children's media property of the time (2000). The playground game expanded on narrative elements provided by Pokemon television programmes, video games, and collecting cards. The children brought together content from across the various media that feature Pokemon, synthesizing these elements in a game of creative make-believe and physical skill. This practice of pastiche recognizes the porousness of media, in that one story world is often deployed across several different delivery platforms. The Pokemon story that the children constructed in their playground game is not dependent upon, nor does it respect, media specificity. Quite the opposite; it purpose-fully defies the distinctions that exist within one property across a range of media and instead draws upon similarities and shared threads of story, character, and action. At the opening of this chapter, the quote from nine-year-old Bill indicates how important the property of Pokemon was at the time the study was conducted. His view of how screen time was allocated across free-to-air TV, video playback, and video game play was structured by his relationship to Pokemon. He seemed to view all the media through the prism of Pokemon. Although Bill admits that he would sometimes tire of the 'Pokemon' video game, when this happened he could easily and happily watch a taped episode of the TV show instead.

Judging by the children's dispassionate views of television in OSHC, relative to the overall media landscape of OSHC, it is fair to say that broadcast or free-to-air television was least important among the media. The children were satisfied with the arrangements as they were and did not request more TV. Other media and other activities were more compelling than television.

Video playback

Like free-to-air television and video games, video playback of movies and pre-recorded television programmes also rely on the TV monitor as screen. Outside of managing the monitor's use across media, the regu-lation of video playback in OSHC is relatively simple. Satisfying a wide range in children's taste while also not offending the sensibilities of par-ents is the top priority for staff. While staff are conscious of keeping the content range within limits that will appeal to children and satisfy par-ents, they are less aware of how their implicit management decisions affect children's activities and habits around video use.

Since OSHC is a recreational place, and movies are, in the main, a form of entertainment enjoyed as recreation, movies are not marked as a privileged experience in OSHC. Movies and pre-recorded TV programmes are part of the normal, if not everyday, fare of recreation. The frequency of video playback is structured by the availability of the screen in the first instance. More important, however, is the management of video selection within taste culture.

Keeping video material confined to G and PG movie classifications is a management strategy aimed at limiting complaints from parents. The PG cap maintains a sort of least common denominator within the range of adult views about what is appropriate for children to watch. While at home many children have access to a range of material across the classification spectrum, at OSHC video selection follows a 'play it safe' rule of thumb because not all parents let their children watch TV or movies with M classifications. Emma Lee's and Luke's comments below are typical of the children's views on the differences between video use at home and at OSHC.

> You are not allowed to watch 'M' here or 'MA' or anything, but I am allowed to watch 'M' at home.
>
> (Emma Lee, 11 years old)
>
> Here and school we are only allowed to watch 'G' and 'PG'. At home we are allowed to watch most rated movies up 'til about M15+.
>
> (Luke, nine years old)

From the point of view of OSHC staff, the most important social consideration for video playback is entertaining a large number of children at one time. To ensure that the largest number of children can watch a video, if they choose to, the collections held by services included G and PG titles exclusively. While many children said they watched M-classified movies at home, they did not criticize the relatively limited selection held at OSHC. They were aware that the G and PG titles catered to the younger children and the older children had already adopted a set of distinctions based on an age hierarchy: younger children were not allowed to watch M titles, so OSHC did not have any. Although some of the older children said that they did not watch the OSHC videos because they were for younger children, they did not consider this to be a flaw in programming or policy since there are so many other things to do at OSHC. Those who did comment on the PG restriction also believed that this was a good policy because other material might be frightening to the younger children, even if they themselves were not bothered by it. Such views are not uncommon in censorship debates. People often justify proposals for censorship by pointing to the interests of others, rather than their own. The older children who mentioned a concern for others did so with an air of pride in their superior position to those younger children.

Among the comments children made about the differences in video playback between homes, classrooms, and OSHC, it is clear that in classrooms, video playback is rare and structured by two imperatives. Video is used either to support educational activities, like viewing *A Bug's Life* when studying insects or it is a reward for achievement or good behaviour.

> Mr. M. [teacher] just showed us the news and told us how interesting it is.
>
> (Kayla, eight years old)

> Sometimes [in class] we watch things that some children bring for special play. Some go outside and others stay inside and just watch the videos. We have to earn the [video] time with bonus points.
>
> (Jake, ten years old)

> At school it's only what and when the teacher wants. At home my brother and I select together but he's 'TV King' and usually selects.
>
> (Treades, eight years old)

In homes, hiring a video from the shop is sometimes a reward and often a weekly ritual. In OSHC, however, video playback is usually and regularly one option among many for recreational entertainment. It is not offered as a reward for good behaviour nor is it withheld as a punishment. It is not directly connected with other activities, although, as already explained, it is structured by the availability of a television monitor. Some services regularly schedule video for a particular day of the week. Like cooking on Wednesdays and ball games on Thursdays, movies often have a scheduled day at OSHC and some children look forward to this day.

Overall, the children had few complaints about the movie selection, despite the fact that movies screened at OSHC are not typical of their consumer habits outside OSHC. While some parents might be concerned that video and television are too available at OSHC, they should be comforted to know that viewing at OSHC is more limited than in most homes. The children were aware of the differences between home video use and OSHC video use but they were not critical of these differences.

Their expectations of movies at OSHC are contexutalized by their viewing experience at OSHC and the children for whom the rules were quite different at home were understanding of the constraints at OSHC.

An active audience

As the game of Playground Pokemon demonstrates, a well-known brand that is visible across different media gives children rich material that they can integrate in other play or which generates play. Barbie, for instance, exists in so many forms, from dolls to books, videos, games, clothing, and so on, that it is the idea of Barbie that becomes central to play and not any one instance of Barbie. The medium itself is less important than the idea(s) represented. The way children thought about Pokemon was central to their transfer of Pokemon from screen to playground. But children don't have to move from screen to playground to be physically active in their media use.

The way in which video is integrated with other play is often dependent upon the level of autonomy that the children are given over how they view. While OSHC staff actively managed video playback with respect to content selection and classification guidelines, they were less aware of how other decisions affected video playback. The physical and spatial settings in which children use video and the level of autonomy they have over playback control are equally important in shaping the ways that they 'view.' Given the freedom to come and go as they choose and to use the remote control, children's video playback practices were quite fluid and involved a range of associated activities that were stimulated by the material on screen. The fluid movement and piecemeal viewing that, 13-year-old, Madison describes was not observed at all the services. 'I mostly sit down and watch videos and things generally if they are on, but I don't sit there very long – for the whole movie. I just come in bits and pieces and watch some of it,' she told me. This style of viewing was found only in the services where video was treated informally and children were 'in charge' of video screenings.

One of the larger services had two television sets and three separate rooms. One TV set was dedicated to video playback and television while the other one supported a Nintendo64 system in a small anteroom with bean bag chairs; both systems were in use most of the time. The video playback and broadcast television system was established in a large area, with the television mounted about 1.5 metres (about five feet) from the ground. The VCR was tucked in to a shelf about one metre from the ground, at easy reach for the children. Below the VCR was a cupboard

Figure 6.1 Open plan TV viewing

stacked with videotapes, and the children made their own selections and operated the system for themselves. Children decided when they would put on the video and which one they would watch (see Figure 6.1).

In front of the screen was a carpeted area about three by four metres with a sofa situated on one-perimeter line. While some children sat on the sofa and others were sprawled across its backrest watching movies, others would often dance and sing along with the movie theme songs in the carpeted open space. Having free reign to operate the remote control, the children often rewound the tapes to replay favourite scenes and songs. When a child wanted to watch a tape, they simply had to select one and power-up the gear. Adults were not consulted and they were not needed to operate the video playback. The children could reach the remote and the tapes were kept in an unlocked, low cabinet. As the movie played, children would come and go in a very fluid manner. If a particular scene or tune grabbed someone's attention, the child would wander into the viewing area and watch for a while before returning to craft, woodworking, or other activities that went on beyond the carpeted area but still within the same room. This situation provided children with the greatest level of autonomy compared to other arrangements. Children were allowed to choose the movies, select the time of viewing, stop the video when they liked, and use the remote control during playback. As a consequence of this freedom, and the spatial arrangements in which the screen was situated, watching videos at this service was a lively activity, which often involved dancing, singing, mini-performances, and lots of talk about the movies, actors, and other viewing experiences. In all the services, children would often read books or magazines while 'watching' a movie.

Often, when a musical number would begin, several children would abandon the other activities they were engaged with and gather around on the carpet to join in the dancing. When the song was finished, they would disperse, returning to their respective activities. Such fluid engagement with the movies was encouraged by the spatial arrangement of the room and the freedom to control playback. The video deck and screen were situated in one corner of a very large room. The room extended beyond the carpet and sofa, and the screen was high enough to be seen from a fair distance. The audio would often cue children at a distance to come into the screening area.

The physical space arrangements, with a large open area in front of the screen, allowed video to inspire a range of play activities in addition to 'watching the movie.' A favourite activity was dancing to theme songs and musical scenes. Sometimes this meant imitating the performances in the movie and other times they designed their own choreography, even for background tunes. They used the VCR like a stereo, seemingly more interested in the audio than the video track of a movie.

At the opposite end of the spectrum is the service that offers the movie-making programme (see Chapter 8). This service did not offer television regularly and when videos were in use the children's control over video playback was restricted. Although the TV monitor is used exclusively for free-to-air TV and video playback (no video game console is attached), the TV is mounted on the wall about two metres (seven feet) off the ground with the VCR below, on a shelf at about 1.5 metres high. An adult could just reach the power switch on the TV. The children could not control the VCR or the monitor, and tapes were kept in the office. When a movie was offered, the children would be presented with two options and the selection would be made by vote. The remote control was kept on a high shelf as well. The children's use of video was much more restricted and their behaviour around movies was more sedate, less physical, even reverent.

The reverent viewing style was certainly supported by the spatial arrangements in the room and restrictions on use of the remote control. In addition to these circumstances, this service also maintained other practices around movies that privileged the feature film form. As I describe in detail in Chapter 8, this service was the only one to engage in media production through the movie-making programme.

Some of the services regularly screened video-taped movies on a particular day (or days) of the week. Like the more elaborate cooking projects, these movie screenings would be scheduled and the children knew on which days there would be a movie. The movies were either selected from the service's collection or hired from a shop. Occasionally children would bring tapes from home. At services with more than one TV set, where video games and tapes could be in use simultaneously, if a child brought a video, they would generally put it on straight away after snack. When children brought tapes, they had usually arranged it in advance with the staff and it would be expected. Bringing a tape from home could bestow a certain prestige on a child. The younger ones, five- and six-year-olds, thought they were pretty special when their tape would be viewed at OSHC. For the older children, the prestige factor only applied if they brought a new release that was popular with their peers.

Only the smallest service had some trouble with children bringing tapes from home. Staff reported that younger children occasionally brought tapes from home that were classified M. This was a 'problem' from time to time but they said that it rarely happened twice with the same child because the G-only rule would be explained to the child if such a mistake were made. Perhaps due to its size, this service ran somewhat more informally than the larger services. With fewer than 20 children on a daily basis, they operated like a large neighbourhood playgroup. It is possible that neither the children nor their parents knew the G-only rule, and more public display and circulation of such rules would probably prevent these breaches in the future.

Other differences in video playback practices were driven by the children and not by the adults. The more control the adults held over video playback, the more it resembled corporate distribution and exhibition practices: rotating the selection, scheduled screenings, and relative containment of bodies while viewing. Where adults gave children autonomy over their viewing and playback use, the children engaged in very playful and active viewing practices, including the physical play of dancing, singing, and performing. They often played the same movie several days in a row or replayed particular scenes over and over again. Some children told us they just 'loved' *Edward Scissorhands* and this is why they played it over and over again. The bacchanalian viewing practices that I describe were not universal across the services where children had autonomy. Rather, autonomy and physical space are *co-regulators* of children's video practices; they both contour how children can and do engage with video playback.

One service allowed the children's use of the remote control, although not the independence to choose when they would view a movie; they had to ask if they could put on a tape. In this service, the video playback set-up was on a rolling cart and had to be moved into position for use. It was normally stored off to the side of the room, because during the school day this was the multi-purpose room. When children would ask for a tape, a staff member would roll the cart into position at a 90-degree angle in front of two small sofas. Effectively a triangle was formed between the monitor and the two sofas. There was a carpet on the floor and this was the only area with soft furnishings in a very large service. When the video was not in use, children would sit in this area to read magazines together, play Game Boy, or chat with one another. The sofa corner had a comfy and cosy feel to it and this was accentuated when the video cart was rolled into the space because it created an even more enclosed feeling to the corner. The carpeted space was only about two square metres, not leaving much room for dancing in front of the screen (see Figure 6.2).

In this area, children did not dance to the videos or sing along with the songs. They sat quietly and watched the movies. The space generated a calm feeling that was reflected in the way children watched videotapes. Rather than supporting the physically active viewing observed at other services, here the spatial arrangements and provision

Figure 6.2 Reading and watching TV

of soft furnishings contained activity and generated a restful atmosphere. The fact that other children were often sitting on the sofas, reading magazines or chatting, may have also influenced the way the movies were viewed. Although children here also had the autonomy to control video playback, they did not use video as a jukebox because they really didn't have room for a dance floor.

Contrary to the image of the viewing zombie, these examples demonstrate the possibilities for lively viewing. A number of influences shape the ways in which children use video in recreation, and there are many different viewing modes, depending on the configuration of contributing factors such as space, furnishings, autonomy, and size of the viewing group. Under one set of circumstances, video playback can support physical activity, and given another set of resources, it may support restful relaxation. Overall, the more physically open the viewing area, the more active the children were around video use. The more autonomy they had over playback, the more varied were their practices around video.

If the goal of OSHC is to create an environment different to school *and* home, to give children a special place with special activities, staff might consider varying the physical arrangements of media so that they are different from what is commonly found in homes. If unique value is to be found in child-centred recreational spaces, we need to look for the ways in which we can make these places different from other places. In the next chapter Internet use and interactive game play are examined in detail.

7
Digital Games and the Internet in OSHC

Video game play essentials: Hardware, software, and play space

While conducting the research in 2000 and 2001, video game play always appeared to be in high demand. That is not to say that it was the most popular activity at Out of School Hours Care (OSHC) for the majority of children. It was, however, a favourite activity for a portion of the children in services that supported video game playing cultures. At the service with the most enthusiastic gaming culture, sometimes 12 to 15 children would be gathered around playing video games and waiting for their turn to have a go at the controls. At the same time, the other 45 children would be spread among the outside activities, craft making, cooking, playing dress up, woodworking, helping staff with jobs, reading, and chatting with friends. The high demand on video games was not due to a lack of other options. Video games, for console and personal technologies, are part of the social fabric of contemporary childhood and their importance extends beyond the limits of the screen's frame. Video games and knowledge of video games form part of the social currency of contemporary childhood and are the 'objects' over which childhood is negotiated both with peers and adults.

Although they had little broadcast television at OSHC, the children did not object. Some, however, did share with us their criticism of the management of video game play. At some services the system for signing up to play video games was simply a first come, first served roster. The most eager and avid players would rush from class to sign up for a turn. With limited playing time, this meant that not everyone had a turn each day. The fastest children to the roster sheet inevitably 'got a go,' while the slower movers might find the roster full when they arrived.

Some staff were aware that such a system was unfair and at least two of the services ensured that children did not play video games on consecutive days if others had not yet had one turn in the week. To manage equity in access and limit individual access, at some services each child was restricted to two ten-minute sessions per week.

In part, video game play at OSHC appeared to be in high demand because screen time for games was limited in any given afternoon – never on for more than an hour and a half. Playing games in two-player mode, with ten-minute turns and accounting for shifting players, only ten children will have a turn at the controls over the course of an hour. Ten minutes is a relatively short game experience and many children enjoyed watching the screen play of others as a way to extend the play experience. It also appears to be popular because the children are so close to one another when playing. Sitting together in a large group, close to each other, elbow to elbow with knees popping up in every which way, group video game play at OSHC is dense. It often appears as if there are more children than a head count would verify. At the services with even the most active gaming cultures, the outdoor playgrounds and fields would always be more populated than the indoor spaces which served electronic games, cooking, billiards, craft, dress up, and relaxed socializing.

Social gaming

The nature of video game play at OSHC, where a large group of children is concentrated in a small physical space, gives the illusion of greater popularity and demand than the numbers would bear out. More children played video games at home or at a friend's house on a regular basis than they did at OSHC. Only 64 per cent of children played video games at OSHC, while 80 per cent played at home. Girls played half as much at OSHC as they did at home, while boys with games at home also played at OSHC (see Figure 7.1). Approximately 15 per cent of the children who played video games regularly at OSHC, such as Alex, did not have video games at home. 'My parents think that having a brother is like having a video game machine. If you have a brother, you don't need a video game machine. So we don't have one.' Even with the restricted availability at OSHC, for some children this was the most regular access they had to video games.

Group play is not only dictated by resources relative to demand at OSHC, it is also children's preferred play style. Interviews with OSHC children confirm what other studies have reported: children prefer to play

Where Kids Play Video Games		
	@Home	@OSHC
Girls	78%	35%
Boys	82%	88%

How Kids Play Video Games		
	Alone	In Company
At Home	38%	48%
At OSHC	23%	77%

Figure 7.1   Video game play statistics

video games with companions (Linderoth et al., 2002; Suss et al., 2001; Sutton-Smith, 1986). Video games do hold the potential to be used solitarily, but, like other toys and games, children prefer to play with other people and will do so with video games when given the opportunity. It is neither the individual nor the play object that is most important to play, but rather the social context in which they are found. The social context provided by OSHC, which demands that children play together at video games and computer games, dictates how video games and computers are used and the degree to which a child can exploit the solitary potential of these playthings.

Interestingly, children were twice as likely to play video games alone at home than they were at OSHC (see Figure 7.1). While at home only half the children played with siblings or friends, more than three-quarters played with others at OSHC. One five-and-a-half-year-old girl said she likes to play video games at OSHC because she gets to play with big children and both boys and girls. At home she plays video games alone and is the youngest of seven children; her closest siblings are brothers. Even the most experienced and avid gamers reported that group play is fun because they learn more about playing by watching other players. 'I get to know cheats to the games and when it's my turn I do the cheats that they did.' And some children enjoy the competition and challenge when 'the other person knows what to do. Usually when I play by myself I always win. It's too easy against the computer.' None of these findings are new to game studies, but I am reporting them here to demonstrate how important the social context is to play and how valued the gaming culture is for its participants. What may appear to be a group of children idly watching others is, in fact, a significant feature of the experience and culture of game playing. Group play supports a range of qualities that are generally considered beneficial to children: friendships across age and gender variation, peer tutoring, opportunities to be an expert, and challenge against and from other players. In a European comparative study of children's ICT use, researchers found that the amount of time children spend away from adults was correlated with peer-group media use. 'Finnish children, with higher levels of non-organized, non-adult supervised time, have higher levels of co-use of ICT, whereas Spanish children have less adult-free time and tend to be solitary users [of ICT], although they make more use of arcade games' (Hutchby and Moran-Ellis, 2001: 4). OSHC offers Australian children opportunities for peer-group media use that are not widely available in a suburbanized society.

In order for children to play video games in a group, the way they prefer to play, they need a large and flexible seating space that is not constrained by fixed furniture. As we have seen with television and video playback, the physical setting and space allocated to the activity shapes the activity. Facilitation of group play requires attention to spatial arrangements. The services that had video games set up in a fashion that allowed children to sit in large groups on the floor, with cushions and beanbags, developed the most enthusiastic gaming cultures. Video game consoles have been designed mainly for use in a family lounge room and the design of institutional facilities does not always support the ideal arrangement of hardware and players.

Some services had the television monitors mounted on wheeled carts so that the sets could be moved into storage rooms at the end of the day. These carts were often too tall for good viewing when seated on the floor. To elevate their eye-line, children brought chairs around and placed them in an arc in front of the screen. In an open space with mobile furniture like small chairs and cushions, children can establish their own arrangements and break them down at the end of the day or end of the play session. Solutions like this are common for services that operate in facilities that serve other needs during the school day.

The best hardware arrangements for video game play were those that created a dedicated space for gaming. In one service, the TV, video player, and game console were mounted on a shelving unit, similar to a home entertainment cabinet. This unit was situated at the midpoint of a three-metre square, carpeted area. This large, open area was bounded by sofas on two sides of the carpet, creating right angle lines extending from the screen. The fourth 'wall' of the square opened onto a larger play area that contained a billiard table and foosball table. On the square carpet often more than a dozen children would be seated on the floor playing video games. While the controls are in the hands of two players, the rest would watch and assist by calling out directions or narrating the on-screen events to the others. The atmosphere was like a sporting arena and yet, amidst all this joyful noise, on the nearby sofas other children would read books, play Game Boy in pairs and threes, or socialize with friends. When parents came, children would often invite them to sit on the sofa while they relayed important events of the day or showed them their latest success on a Game Boy.

Some parents expressed concern that the video games were available the entire afternoon and that their child might have been playing for two hours or more. Staff members had a difficult task in explaining to parents why their child was always in the video game area when the parents came by to take him/her home. Some might stay for several turns, their own and those of their friends, but rarely would they sit for more than 40 minutes around the video games. Staff did not allow children to sit around the game console all afternoon. The children usually only stayed around the machine while their friends were playing and then they would run out to the yard or pick up another activity. Sometimes staff would suggest to a child that s/he go outside for a while, if the child had been playing and watching others play video games for what appeared to be a long time. When they were asked to go outside or do something else, the children cooperated without vocal or visible objection and never came back to the game that same day. It is possible that such staff interventions were prompted by expressed parental concern but this was not obvious in the delivery. Ad hoc regulation of this sort was in addition to the timed turns at the controls. Such intervention was also often stimulated by the noise level that the children were generating around the video game play. When it would get 'out of control' (too loud for the adults or other children), staff might say that video games were coming to an end for the day and the players would quickly find something else to do, often relocating to discuss the day's game play or other games.

In a service that is small in attendance and in physical space, the video game machine was set up in a corner that had two small sofas for sitting and a small, carpeted area where four or five children could sit on the floor. Here too the video game play was joyful and enthusiastic even though the space was less than two square metres. Players with the controls usually would sit on the floor and the onlookers would be seated on the sofa behind them. A particularly crowded session would have other children behind the sofa, standing to view the on-screen play. Everyone appeared comfortable and the space accommodated ten children easily.

Although video game consoles have been designed for use with a television set (ideally in a family home) when television sets are scarce, a computer monitor is a ready substitute. Two services have taken up this option since they have only one TV. Using old and relatively small, 'hand-me-down' computer monitors, video game systems are connected to the computer hardware suite. The smaller monitor takes up less space and seems like a good idea for small areas. While this hardware arrangement does free up the television monitor for other media delivery and allows game play to occur in close quarters, it also changes the social dynamic around video game play and does not support group play very well.

Since the computer monitors are small, in order to see the images and action clearly, players sit much closer to the screen than they do when playing video games on a larger television monitor. In addition, the smaller computer monitor is usually situated on a standard classroom table. Thus the size and placement of the monitor requires players to sit in chairs to easily and comfortably view the screen action. If players sat on the floor and looked up at the computer monitor on the table, their eye-line would not be convenient to the horizon of the screen and they would probably become uncomfortable. Sitting further back might be a solution, but with the smaller screen size, it is not desirable to sit further away from the screen because a player might miss a cue in the game play. Sitting on chairs has the advantage of allowing the players the best view of the screen action, but it also has its drawbacks. While seated on chairs, fewer children can gather around the screen at one time because the chairs themselves take up more space on the viewing arc. Generally, children's bottoms are smaller than the seats and the chair legs also extend a bit from the seat width. Ultimately, sitting on chairs takes up an additional 8 cm (3.5 inches) per player. It effectively reduces by one-quarter the number of players who can comfortably sit 'in front' of the screen. If the chairs were not required to view the screen, I doubt that they would have used them since they sat on the floor for many other activities without complaint.

Two of the services utilized an arrangement like this, with computer monitors on tables and video game controls connected to them. At one site, the monitors sat on a table squashed in so closely to an air hockey table that there was barely enough room for two chairs in front of the screen. Children could not gather around behind the players to watch the game because they would risk being elbowed by an air hockey player. In this setting it was rare to see more than four children together at the video game.

At the other service, the set-up was a secondary gaming area. The primary gaming area was a cosy corner with a sofa and rug where a game machine was connected to a television mounted on a wheeled cart. The children would sit on the sofa or the floor a bit more than a metre (about four feet) from the screen. The secondary gaming area, the one utilizing computer monitors, was against a wall with the screens facing out to an open area. The chairs backed up to this open space and children could easily stand behind seated players and view screen action. In this configuration, there was room to move chairs and bodies so that the viewing arc could be expanded to accommodate several children playing in a group. The children usually set up the chairs in rows parallel to the screen, like a theatre setting. Two to four seats would make up the row closest to the screen; the next row had six seats and the third would have eight. Behind the seated players several more could stand and look over the shoulders of the seated players. Although the computer screen can serve as the monitor for video games, the small screen makes it more difficult for large numbers of children to see the screen well; the larger television screen provides a better view for more children and thus group play is supported and tacitly encouraged.

Software and gaming platforms

Providing a comfortable gaming environment where groups of children can play video games is ideal but it is not sufficient. The software selection must also appeal to a wide range of children, accounting for the preferences of age and gender. The games must be challenging enough to merit replay and they must also meet with parental approval. Fulfilling these requirements for children who range in age from 5 to 12 is not easy. Fortunately, some of the work of software selection is done by the market. At the time the study was conducted, the greatest range of titles for children in the OSHC age group was made for the Nintendo range of systems and its associated Game Boy. The services with the most active gaming cultures had in common the Nintendo64 gaming platform and a selection of software that included 'MarioKart,' 'Mario Party,' 'Diddy Kong Racing,' 'Pokemon Stadium,' and 'Banjo-Kazooie' among other less popular titles. The 'Mario' and 'Pokemon' games were popular with both boys and girls, and love for the characters was often cited by girls as a central appeal in the games: 'I like playing 'Pokemon Stadium' because I have the soft toys and figures.' When the children selected a 'make-believe name' for their interview, several of them took on character names such as Mew and Mario. The 'Pokemon' phenomenon was at the height of its popularity when the interviews were conducted, and the video games, videotapes, trading cards, and other playthings were almost universally popular with boys and girls. Mario has been a mainstay of children's video gaming culture for many years and is also popular with girls and boys alike.

Many of the Nintendo64 titles are also available for Game Boy and the replication across platforms can enhance the gaming culture when Game Boys are part of the OSHC media landscape. One service had six Game Boys, and children were also allowed to bring their own hand-held devices from home. Children often commented that they liked going into the box and selecting a Game Boy cartridge from among a wide selection. Choosing was part of the fun. The other services did not provide Game Boys but did allow children to use them if they brought them from home. Some schools, however, did not allow Game Boy devices at all, and some parents did not want their children to bring the Game Boy to OSHC, for fear that they would be lost or damaged. Where there were Game Boys in play, children often would play with friends, two or three gathered around one Game Boy. Even this 'personal' technology can be utilized for social purposes in gregarious play, sometimes even stimulating group play.

PlayStation games were available at two of the services. At one this was the secondary gaming area, in addition to the more primary Nintendo64 station. At the other service, PlayStation was the only gaming platform, and the Service Director complained that the selection of games on the market was not the best but that the hardware had been donated to the service and they could not afford to change it at the time. Here the children had a selection of games in roughly two genres, driving games and dance performance. The driving games included 'Rollcage' and 'Formulae 198.' The dancing games were 'Busta Groove' and 'Spice Girls.' Although the selection was limited, both boys and girls played across the genres. The children were also allowed to bring their Game Boys from home although the service did not provide any.

Where PlayStation was a secondary gaming platform, the games were mainly played by boys and included 'Crook,' 'Burning Roads,' 'Crash Bandicoot,' 'Grand Tourismo,' 'Formula 1,' and the skateboarding simulation, 'TonyHawk,' which was the most popular at the time. As described earlier, the PlayStation systems were set up with computer monitors as display screens. Although this set-up did allow several children to gather around, the selection of software was not very appealing to the girls and they rarely took a turn at the controls. Occasionally girls would watch the play from the outer edge of the viewing arc but they did not stay long. A particularly noisy cheer from the playing group could draw the attention of children doing other things nearby but their attention to the play was fleeting and they would return to their drawing, board games, dancing, or continue on their way outside (the station was near the exit to the playground).

Management and the active gaming culture

The main 'problem' with video games seems to be their popularity. Without an active gaming culture, video games do not present a problem. Precisely what makes them popular also can be troublesome. The sounds coming from the games are important to their appeal and to their play, but it is often the noise, from the game and the players, that draws criticism from adults and other children. There are several strategies for reducing the volume of game play. The simplest solution is to turn the monitor volume down or off. Another solution is to provide headsets for players but this option does not suit group play. Two sets of earphones or headsets can provide two players with audio enrichment but it divides the group into players with audio access and observers without. Headsets are better utilized when an individual wants to be isolated from the larger activity. The appeal of group play is that one is not isolated, but rather is part of the larger group whether controlling screen action or observing and advising on play.

To contain video game play and keep the noise to a minimum, one service invested in carpeting a small alcove and outfitted the room with beanbag chairs and the Nintendo set-up with a television. The monitor faced an open door leading onto the playground. The acoustics of the small room contained the audio spill of the enthusiastic game play to a satisfactory level. Refitting this small space to cater for video game play required a minor financial investment but more importantly it required a positive attitude towards video game play.

In the three services with enthusiastic gaming cultures, the staff did not view video game play as less respectable than other forms of play or other activities. Staff saw video game play as a legitimate leisure-time activity for children because it was what the children wanted to do.

Staff often purchased games on the recommendation of children. This ensures that game purchases are (cost) effective and it engenders positive feelings in the child about self, OSHC, and OSHC staff. Children often comment positively about school or OSHC having something that they have at home. Children feel special when OSHC has some correspondence with home. In the single service that provided several Game Boys, the Service Director had purchased them when she saw how popular the Nintendo64 was. She viewed the addition of Game Boys as a way to relieve some of the pressure of demand from the console game. She was correct.

In one of the services with a poorly developed gaming culture, it was limited resources and limited space that interfered with a better development of the gaming culture. This service had a hand-me-down PlayStation and very few games. The children enjoyed the limited selection and were allowed to bring games from home within the G classification but the service could not afford to provide a larger selection of games. Despite an inability to invest in media resources, staff expressed a comfortable ease when talking with the children about video games and the related play of card collecting. In this working class suburb, all but one of the children had at least one game console at home and most had more than one.

In the other service with a poorly developed gaming culture, the Service Director had a negative opinion of video games and did not like a group of children to gather around the video game station. The restrictions on group play and the poor equipment and spatial arrangements made playing video games unpleasant for the children. They simply chose to do other things because video gaming was not fun under these circumstances. No effort was made by staff to enrich the gaming environment for comfort and accessibility. Video games were connected to a computer monitor and positioned in a tight corner abutting the air hockey table. There were other spaces where video game consoles could have been situated for better playing access but since video games were viewed as a 'waste of time,' adults did not make their placement a priority. Despite my disappointment in the situation, the children did not express objection to the arrangements and they seemed to accept the circumstances or, at least, they did not expect anything different.

The most common problem that the children and staff had with video game play was monitoring individual access, or making sure everyone who wanted a turn got a chance to play with the controls. Even with ten-minute turn limits, keeping track of whose turn was next sometimes presented confusion. This was not a challenge for the smallest service but in the larger ones, with active gaming cultures, sometimes 20 children would want to play video games on a given day. These services established a roster system for turns. Children would write their names down on a list, either on paper or on a blackboard, and when their turn was complete they would hand over the controls to the next player. Two problems occurred with this system. In one service the youngest children, five- and six-year-olds, could not tell time. They had no idea what a ten-minute-turn meant. Much to our amusement, we observed arguments over turn length in which neither of the disputants knew how to tell time. In another service the staff purchased several small alarm clocks to assist the children in timing their turns. The clocks would invariably be broken, and staff suspected that the damage was not always accidental. Another problem with a paper roster is simply keeping it.

> You're only allowed to play Nintendo64 once a week and I think it should be twice a week. Then you could do it on Monday and Friday. If they lose the list, then they just start a new list. Everybody who's on the old list gets to go again. It's good if they lose the list!
>
> (Bill, 9 years old)

The blackboard roster appeared to work better than the paper roster because it was kept in public view. Like all management, regulating turns is work. In any given week, if all children are to get one turn before anyone gets a second turn, a degree of vigilance is necessary to ensure that the system is adhered to. Making the roster public results in less adult intervention because social surveillance is more generalized among the children and staff. Children can actively participate in the management of turns when the roster is publicly posted. For the children who cannot read well enough to monitor the roster and ensure their own stake, there was always at least one older child who took pleasure in being on the lookout for the interests of younger children.

The demand for video game play and the provision of accessible gaming areas were also dependent upon the balance of other activities. Computer access drew considerable interest from girls, and in services with greater computer access there was considerably less demand for video games.

Computers, software, and Internet access

Where services varied the most was in their provision of computers, peripherals, and Internet access. Services with access to the school's computer network or lab were able to offer the greatest access to a large number of computer terminals, printers, software, and the Internet. One service regularly had access to the computer lab one day per week. One large service, with attendance around 55 children per day, had daily computer access. Consequently, they had more staff members and were able to disperse the children among several, independent locations and still maintain requisite supervision ratios. The school's computer lab was one of the places they used every day.

The 'homework club' met in the computer lab after sign-in and snack. Mondays through Thursdays, older children (Grades Five to Seven) were supposed to spend the first half-hour of the session doing their homework. This policy was instituted at the request of parents and unique among the services studied. Younger children whose parents wanted them to practise reading or do other studying were also allowed to participate in homework club. As a reward for having done their homework, the children had free use of the computers for the rest of the afternoon. The younger children were also allowed to use the computer room at the end of the homework session. On Fridays the computer room was available for all to use and homework club did not operate.

Computers lined three of the walls, monitors facing into the centre. There were 15 computer stations and room enough for two chairs at each station. This physical design, with monitors around the perimeter of the room but facing inwards, has long been recommended as the best arrangement for children's classroom use because it offers the greatest screen visibility for teachers and peers. It is also an excellent arrangement for monitored recreation of the sort that OSHC provides. While there is little official 'teaching' at OSHC, there is plenty of peer tutoring around games and computer use. The open arrangement also allows staff to monitor the screens, a need that has arisen with greater access to the Internet's wealth of content.

In the centre of the room, several tables were arranged in a square and this served as the homework table for those who were doing work that did not require a computer. There was a colour printer, and all the computers were networked to the school's server system and the Internet. A wide variety of 'educational' games on CD ROM were available to the children. On any given day, you could find several children playing 'SimCity,' mini-golf, researching their favourite collectibles, playthings, movies, television shows, sports teams, and game cheats on the Internet, and a quarter of them would be doing school projects (see Figure 7.2).

Access to the school's network meant that children who wanted to work on their school projects could do so for as long as they liked. Boys mainly used the OSHC computers for going online and this often meant

Figure 7.2   Computer room

playing games. Girls, on the other hand, used the OSHC computers for a wider variety of activities. Their use was more evenly distributed across game playing, schoolwork, and Internet use than was reported by the boys. Comparing computer use at OSHC with use at home, four times as many girls used OSHC computers for schoolwork. Among the boys, game playing on computers was more common at home than at OSHC, despite the greater Internet access at OSHC. These findings suggest that when given a greater range of options, children will engage in activities across the spectrum of offerings. Having the software and files for their school projects, the printers, and Internet access, the children used the computers for more than game play. At home, many children use the computer for only game play.

The younger children tended to use the computers in pairs and threes, while the older children often pursued their tasks alone but still sought engagement from their peers. These notes were taken by one of the researchers during an observation session:

> Three girls, who cannot even reach the floor with their feet, sit by their computers and play interactive educational games, while someone on the other side of the room is building up a world in 'SimCity'. Someone increases the volume on the machine to attract attention.

A young boy asks a girl for advice on how to throw a 'dyna-stick' in a game. A girl dances to Calypso music coming from her computer and she spins back and forth next to the computer. Some other children are screaming into a little microphone, sampling their voices into the computer.

Apart from the younger children (mostly boys) who are completely engulfed by the screen they share with a number of their friends, everyone is playing alone. And all those loners are doing something to get attention from the other children: raising the volume, doing a little computer dance, asking for tips, trying to impress with what they have achieved etc. It seems that the end result for all those solitary computer users actually is social interaction with the other people in the room.

(24 October 2001)

While there were enough computers for each child to pursue an independent task, unless children were doing a school project, they sought feedback, support, approval, and companionship in their recreational computer use. When surfing the Internet, for example, children would often want to share their discoveries with others, and we often observed two children sitting at adjacent computers, each searching for something different but regularly calling to the other to have a look at what had been found or what was new on a site that they both knew well.

There are several features of the school's computer lab that make it a valuable asset to OSHC. First of all, the children are familiar with the hardware and software set-up. They know how it all works and what the system will support. In this school, a firewall and filtering system are in place, and each child has an account for school-associated use of the Internet. This relieves OSHC staff from the burden of monitoring web access. Since the computers are networked to a server, the children have access to the software and files they use for their schoolwork. If they wish to do homework or research for a class project, all the materials are readily at hand. This is especially important for children who do not have computers at home or for whom the home computer is incompatible with the school's system. This is the case for nearly 25 per cent of all children. At this school, however, 90 per cent of the children have computers at home, but most reported using the home computer for game play and seldom for schoolwork. Only 20 per cent used computers at home for schoolwork, while at OSHC, by contrast, 55 per cent used the computers for schoolwork. The most popular activities were web browsing and game play but schoolwork rated third at OSHC.

At home, few children had access to the Internet. At OSHC, when Internet access is part of the established suite of tools and opportunities, they all have access. Although only three of the six services in the study had access to the Internet, the children reported using the Internet at OSHC twice as often as they did at home. Many children also do not have the same software at home and do not transfer files between classroom and home, so computer access at OSHC provides an opportunity to work on school assignments outside class time. For many children, OSHC is the only access point for such activities. This is not to suggest that children should spend their recreational hours doing what is effectively their work, school assignments. The point I am making here is that when children do find their computer-based schoolwork engaging and even compelling, it is advantageous for them to have a place where they can pursue this interest at their leisure. Using computers for school assignments at OSHC should not preclude parents from participating in children's schooling by supporting their lessons at home. But it is important to recognize that when an OSHC service provides children with access to the school's computer network, children are given access to more than the software and hardware. It is the social environment of OSHC that shapes the experience of computer use. Working on school assignments during OSHC time and space is a different experience than working on those same assignments in class time and space.

Two of the services that provided Internet access were large services but one had access to the school's computer lab, while the other had four computers in a small alcove room, apparently a former storage closet. The third service with Internet access was very small and had only one computer. Where the children had access to the school's computer lab, 71 per cent of the children used the Internet at OSHC, while only 43 per cent used the Internet at home. At the service with just four computers, 54 per cent of the children used the Internet at OSHC and only 29 per cent used it at home. The lower figures for home use are not surprising considering parents are often wary of children using the Internet because they are unsure how to use and install filtering software or take other safety measures (ABA, 2005). Among those without Internet access at home, all of them reported using the Internet at OSHC. In the third service, the computer was not often used by the children. This was in part due to the physical circumstances of the computer placement. Only two children could sit comfortably at the computer because it was literally housed in a closet.

Another large service did not have access to the school lab nor did it have any recent model hardware. Instead, it had eight Commodore64 stations. Each station was equipped with a suite of different games, and the children knew which games were stored on which terminal. The Commodores were lined up against a wall and sat idle most of the time. The most use they ever had was from a couple of five-year-olds. When I asked other children if they ever played with these games, most simply replied, 'no.' The few who offered more extensive comments were critical: 'I don't use them because they're boring. The games on there, I don't think are very good.' Good games were described as 'games that are on more modern computers with better graphics.' The most condemning assessment was offered by a child using the pseudonym 'Mew,' after one of the Pokemon characters:

> They've got dodgy games, very dodgy games. They're probably the dodgiest I've ever seen, probably better than nothing. They're not in the latest fashion and they don't work properly. A better computer, the newest computer out, the ones with the colored bubbles and the circle mouse you turn them on at the keyboard.

One child did not even recognize the Commodore as a computer, 'I don't really know if they have them [computers]. I don't think they do,' he told me when I asked if he ever used the computers at OSHC. It is wise, however, to keep in mind that these computers were presented to the children as game machines. They only had game software, and the service also had an active Nintendo and Game Boy culture. It is not surprising that these 'collectible' games would be viewed by young children without the respect and nostalgia that they might inspire in adults who knew these games as their first. These children criticize the graphics and action of the games because their standard of comparison is the 3D game graphic and action of later gaming technologies.

At a large service with only four computers situated in the former broom closet, a core group of young boys (aged 7 to 9) usually played at the computers. We often saw two or three children playing games from packaged software and another child online. One of the concerns that staff had was the children's unmonitored access to the Internet. While staff could see the children in the room, they could not see the computer screens. They worried that the children were sometimes venturing into websites that would not normally be considered 'for children.' Our observations, however, did not confirm these suspicions. It is, of course, possible that the presence of adult research staff might have been a signal for children to be on their 'best behavior.' During our visits, the most common online activities for boys were playing games or searching the web for video game cheats. Girls spent a lot of time looking at 'gossip' sites, finding information about pop stars, and details on dolls, animals, and other collectibles that were popular at the time. Both boys and girls would share their Internet information with others when they reconvened in a group. In the same way that boys would demonstrate their knowledge of games by citing the latest cheat that they had discovered online, girls would share information about collectibles (i.e. citing the latest release in a series or talking about the features of a collectible item). Neopets, the online equivalent of a Tamogachi, were also popular at the time and of interest to the girls at this service. They would visit the site daily to feed and care for their virtual pets.

The other large service with limited computer access took a very innovative approach to increasing access. Their solution was to jointly purchase two laptop computers, sharing the cost with the school. During school hours, the laptops were used in classrooms and at the end of the day, they would be carried over to OSHC. The laptops were outfitted with the same software as the children used in school and they were able to connect to the school's server from OSHC. The service had only just acquired the laptops when the study was underway.

In the very small and relatively poor service, the sole computer was equipped with word processing software, some games, and Internet connectivity. The computer was kept in a closet, fitted with a desk. When the closet door was open, two children could bring chairs to the desk and use the computer together. The computer, however, was not in high demand. Children mainly used it for looking up things on the Internet, drawing pictures, and playing games, most often individually rather than with friends, perhaps because the space was so cramped. Since the study was conducted, the service has acquired more space and moved the administration desk to their new space. They now have room for a computer station for the children. The physical set-up is much more appealing, the computer situated on a modified U-shaped table, at the periphery of the main room. Several children can gather around the table and view the screen as a group, and staff can observe the screen from several vantage points within the room. Staff say that the computer is used more frequently now.

Finally, another medium-sized service did not have any computer access for two reasons. Firstly, there was no Internet connectivity in their building. The service operated out of a portable building that was scheduled for refitting and refurbishing. They were awaiting the renovations before making any substantial investment in computers but then the building plans were delayed. This service also had limited physical space and allocating a section to create computer stations was not a priority. Their priority was in video production and movie-making. Funds that other services might have spent on computer stations were here allocated to the movie production programme (see Chapter 8).

When we began research, none of the services had filtering or blocking software. Even when one service acquired a system, OSHC staff still felt an obligation to monitor the children's Internet access. Staff brought the issue of monitoring to our attention and we subsequently incorporated this as a research interest. The staff who brought this to our attention worked at the service where the computers were in a former broom closet, monitors facing the interior, and out of staff view. Given the relative privacy that the children had in this space, staff thought that the children might not always practice the self-regulation that they had been taught. From time to time, staff would step in to the computer room to have a look. Mainly, though, they relied on the children's ability to self-regulate and for peer monitoring to have some regulatory effect either in the form of surveillance or by children 'dobbing in' their mates.[1] Given that daily attendance was over 35 children, the few instances that staff could offer as examples of children breaching the rules demonstrate that the peer surveillance and clear guidelines for use worked well. The children knew the rules and followed them, despite the ongoing anxiety that adults held about Internet use. Or the children kept their transgressions secret, perhaps more cause for adult anxiety.

At the large service with daily access to the school's computer lab, while a staff member was always present in the lab, management relied on self- and peer regulation. Since monitors faced the room's centre, staff were able to view any screen at any time. They were also secure in their belief that most children would not break the rules and that if rules were broken, another child would report it. Ironically, the biggest problem they experienced occurred when the school adopted a firewall system with filtering and blocking software.

The school gave each child a personal, password-protected account, and the children were told that they each had five dollars worth of Internet use. The children were supposed to do their schoolwork with this account and were allowed to use the remainder as they chose, within the established rules of use and as allowed by the filtering and blocking software. They were not supposed to go to 'rude' sites or send email messages with nasty words in them. Within a week of the system's implementation, several children had depleted their accounts. They had been playing graphically intense online games at OSHC and their funds were devoured.

Nobody, staff included, knew how this happened because they did not know how use was calculated as dollars. The software counted use in bits. Bits had a price. Downloading the graphic-heavy games meant transferring a lot of bits. Consequently their accounts were emptied. When they were denied access, the children would come to OSHC staff and say, 'I only went to one site,' or 'I was only on for ten minutes.' The children calculated use as experience, how many places they 'went' on the Internet or the duration of their stay at the sites. They conceived use in terms of geography (places visited) and time (time online). It had not occurred to the children or adults that Internet use was being calculated as volume, in bits. It was only when several children had their accounts depleted that staff found out how the system worked. Even after learning this, there were still some children who had problems because when a game site was accessed, there was no indication of the bit volume that would be transferred in the process of bringing the game to life on the screen. The OSHC Director was quick to respond once the issue was understood. OSHC established their own account so that the children did not have to use their individual school accounts for game play. This solved the problem in time for the next school-holiday session when many of the children at Vacation Care would spend time playing online games and feeding their Neopets.

The filtering and blocking software also had a surveillance function, and children delighted in telling us about how other children had written nasty words or rude emails and been caught. According to the children, when someone was caught, s/he had to see the principal. Since the stories were always about someone else, and the nasty words changed with each telling of the story, these tales may be school-sized 'urban myths.' Nevertheless the circulation of such stories serves a function of surveillance by establishing and maintaining a presence of surveillance, despite its historical truth. The children believed that others had been caught and their stake in the possibility of surveillance was large enough that they told researchers about it.

Even though passive surveillance seems to work well in these communities, posting rules and regulations in plain view within the computer use areas is always a good idea. Posting the rules of use establishes a common ground for all the users and serves as a declaration from the service that management is aware of how children can ensure that their time online is pleasant and in keeping with community standards and expectations. Similar to the variation in family practices around video content, rules about Internet and computer use also vary and we cannot assume that children know the basic rules of online safety. Even if they have been instructed on the safe use at home or at school, posting a reminder is a simple way to assist them in their own self-regulation.

Media and play: Finding the balance

The overarching goal of OSHC is to provide a safe and pleasant recreational space for children's leisure time. Services seek to achieve this goal by providing a balance of activities, so that children can choose from among a wide range of indoor and outdoor, group and individual activities. But what is safe and enjoyable for a 12-year-old may not appeal to a five-year-old and what is reasonable for an older child may not be deemed so for a younger child. Among the range of activities that OSHC services provide, media in particular highlight the challenge in creating a varied programme of activities that are both popular and 'safe.' While adults believe that children will self-select appropriately among other activities, they do not believe that children are very good at selecting, self-monitoring, and self-regulating their media play. Moreover, adults are not often concerned that children might be spending too much time drawing or playing physically active games but they are concerned with the amount of time that children give to electronic media of all types. While adults recognize the value and pleasure that children derive from media, they often struggle with whether or not this pleasure is appropriate leisure. At heart, many adults still view media play as inferior to other forms of play. Finding an acceptable balance among the activities that children enjoy, including media play, is a heavy burden on adults. The good news is that, in OSHC, the burden of management is dispersed across several levels of regulation and adults need not feel that this responsibility is theirs alone.

In the social environment of OSHC, where children are always among the company of their peers, and individual media compete with one another for screen time and space, the limited resources and high demand combine to limit children's individual access to media and make media play a group activity. This combination of circumstances, however, does not provide sufficient management or regulation of media use and should not be a substitute for other proactive practices.

Free-to-air television use is restricted by the broadcasting schedule itself. The limited selection of programmes that appeal to children in the post-school hours makes television an unappealing option in the

OSHC hours. If services were to subscribe to pay TV (satellite or cable), the range of attractive programming might raise the level of interest from children, especially since so few Australian households have pay TV. It would appeal not only for the variety it provides but also for its novelty or special status as something that 'only OSHC has.' Simply put, television would become more appealing to children and consequently it would become a greater management burden for staff.

The appeal of video use in OSHC is increased with the level of autonomy that children are given over playback circumstances. Allowing children to select the videos for themselves, turn on the player, and use the remote were all factors that increased the appeal of video in OSHC and made its use more varied. Autonomy over video playback, as I have shown, stimulated a range of activities as accompaniment to the video. Physical activity and creative performance were both stimulated by video playback when the independence to use video in these ways was allowed, and when space accommodated the physical activities. Providing a library of videos for the children to select from, at their leisure, was shown to be an excellent practice. It allows adults to control the range of choice but not the act of choice. At the services that used this system, we did not observe any conflict around video playback but we did observe greater variety and more activity around video playback. Providing children with the freedom to select video playback at will, however, was dependent upon having another television monitor to support video games because demand for video games was usually strongest between the two activities.

Video game play at OSHC is the most regulated media activity because its popularity creates a demand that cannot be met without some system to ensure that the resource is shared fairly among the children. A system or set of guidelines is necessary to ensure that each child who wants a turn gets one. Time limits on turns and group play are the methods that best meet this need. But how turn taking was enforced differed from service to service with varying levels of success. Allowing group play also helps ease the pressure on the scarce resources of screen time and generates more turns per afternoon session as children play simultaneously. More importantly, group play is the way children prefer to play video games, and for many, OSHC is the only place where they have this pleasure.

Facilitating the roster of players is an aspect of management where most services could improve video game play. Having a publicly posted roster, on a white board or chalkboard, is one option. Taking a few minutes at the start of the session to help children sign up and posting the list publicly helps to ensure equity for the younger and slower children who might not rush to the game console upon arrival. If the roster is established with an announcement, everyone has an equal chance of getting their name down.

Time limits on turns also need monitoring. As we observed, some children are not very good at telling time, and still others are not very keen on keeping time accurately. One solution would be to select an official timekeeper each afternoon. This child could have charge of a stopwatch or clock and be responsible for ensuring fair play. Given the number of children who enjoy participating in video game play as spectators, it might not be too difficult to encourage such a role as part of video game play at OSHC. It is already quite different to video game play elsewhere, so it shouldn't be too difficult to institute child-directed regulation of this sort.

The greatest management challenge with respect to computer use was to ensure that children did not visit websites that were outside the guidelines of acceptability. As more services gain access to computers and the Internet, this concern will become more generalized. While I am not an advocate of filtering and blocking software, services and schools will be adopting such software as part of service packages, including firewall protection and networking. Filtering and blocking software do nothing to encourage children's abilities to self-regulate and self-manage their Internet use. These applications build virtual garden walls in which to contain children. They limit children's opportunity to actively evaluate their own practices by acknowledged criteria. As we have seen, peer surveillance is quite effective in the public setting and OSHC computer use is public and social on the whole. Where it is not public and social, it ought to be. Computer screens should be in public view, and guidelines or rules for use should be publicly posted, so that when children are reminded of the rules the oral instruction is reinforcement of prior knowledge.

Although it may not be the right of adults to insist that child's play be productive, this is a burden that child's play often carries. The next chapter describes Movie Magic, a movie-making programme that engaged children in media production.

8
Making Media

'Edutainment' – A useful metaphor

Suggesting a generic category that blurs the boundary between education and entertainment by marshalling entertainment in the service of education and learning, the term, 'Edutainment' entered our vernacular in the mid-1990s. Around the time that Microsoft's Windows Operating Systems took firm hold of the domestic consumer market in personal computers, Edutainment described an important software category. With the home hardware market firmly secured, the next step was to ensure that these machines would remain relevant in the domestic context. Marketing of software was essential to meeting this need and Edutainment – software that would help children learn useful things while they played – was one of the pillars of this campaign. Edutainment titles were most often games to develop literacy and maths skills and this appealed to parents especially. One of the most popular of these titles was 'Math Blaster' in the 1990s; more recent standouts include 'Blues Clues,' 'Pajama Sam: No Need to Hide,' 'Spy Fox: Operation Ozone,' 'Freddie Fish 3: Stolen Conch,' and 'The Logical Journey of the Zoombinis.'

Edutainment is the notional space, the place where education and entertainment meet, and it provides a useful metaphor for thinking about the possibilities for media education that can occur in Out of School Hours Care (OSHC). Like Edutainment, OSHC services blend elements from two distinct spheres, home and classroom, in the creation of a distinct hybrid space. Elsewhere (Chapter 3 and Vered, 2001) I have characterized OSHC and its relationship to the social spaces of home and classroom as 'intermediary space.' The metaphor of Edutainment also neatly describes the type of media learning that goes on in OSHC, where children learn things by participation in recreational activities that more closely resemble play than classroom curriculum.

Children's play, whether it is with media or more traditional play things and scenarios, involves understanding and interpreting stories, engaging in activities, and manipulating objects (including virtual ones). In more expansive play, children generate and create stories, activities, and objects. They often take the familiar characters and storylines supplied by mass media and modify them, spin them, and fashion their own versions with creative flair, as I have described in previous chapters. Almost all of us can recall a childhood game that required imitating a well-known character or story from popular culture. For some, these may first have been known through media that pre-date television, video, and computer games, such as comic books and radio. Children today not only dress up and perform the roles of superheroes and popular music artists but they can also record their performances (play) in a number of media formats with readily available consumer technologies. (For recent work on pre-teen girls, radio, and musical performance see essays by Sarah L. Baker, 2001, 2004a, 2004b.)

Edutainment suggests that production and consumption are not neatly separate activities but that children's media play, when viewed as productive activity, is intimately associated with models and conventions of entertainment. Rather than regarding children's media play as exclusively consumptive and dismissing its creative value, the metaphor of Edutainment turns our attention to the dual practices of production and consumption. By taking a close look at media production in OSHC, I will demonstrate how qualities implied in the notion of Edutainment – education and entertainment, or learning through and with models from the entertainment industries – are deployed in creative media production activities outside the classroom.

Media recreation/education

After long debate, it is now widely accepted (if not always practised) that media education programmes should include production exercises and projects, in addition to the critical analysis of media, because, among other reasons, people learn best by doing. In making movies, children can learn about media production and media products in a process that allows them to apply their considerable fan and consumer knowledge to a unique production project. As children draw upon their consumer and fan practices to make movies, they demonstrate the practice of knowledge scaffolding. By informing production activities with the implicit knowledge gained through consumer and fan practices, entertainment becomes a means for education. Children learn about media production through reflection on their consumer practices and these, in turn, inform their production experiences and the products they make. But, as David Buckingham points out in *Media Education: Literacy, Learning and Contemporary Culture* (2003), the constraints of formal education can encumber this process because the demand to meet curriculum requirements and demonstrate educational outcomes does not always fit neatly with recreation-based production programmes. Despite Buckingham's continued recognition and support for children's informal media education, the emphasis in *Media Education* is weighted towards the more formal, school-based media education programmes in secondary years. In the section, 'Media Education beyond the Classroom,' several locations are identified as providing media education outside schools but recreational care services are not among them (pp. 99–101). I view this omission as an invitation to consider the type of media education opportunities that childcare services can provide for young children, between the ages of 5 and 12.

The media mix

Among the six services in the study, five allowed children open, yet regulated, access to video, free-to-air television, video games, and computers. By comparison, one service was relatively conservative. Computers were not available; video game play was closely monitored; the selection of games was small, and use was restricted. The TV set was used primarily as a monitor for video screenings of popular children's films, while free-to-air television was rare (see Chapters 6 and 7). Although cut-outs of popular media characters decorated the walls and children played with sticker books and magazines related to movies and popular culture, the children were generally encouraged to spend their leisure time on outdoor play, games, craft, reading, and socializing rather than playing video games or watching TV. The two computers on hand did not appeal to the children because the software was extremely limited and the hardware quite old. Overall, the breadth of entertainment media that were so popular at other services were not significant in the programming here.

Movies, however, in the commercial and spectacular senses of the term, what we might call 'the Hollywood ideal,' were quite important (and still are).[1] The OSHC Service Director has a fondness for movies. He often sets up a large screen in one of the adjacent halls and projects

DVD movies in darkness, replicating the movie-going experience. In the school holidays, when the service runs its Vacation Care Program, these events become more elaborate with children being issued mock movie tickets for admission to the screenings and special snacks such as popcorn added to the usual fare of Vegemite sandwiches and fruit. A particular combination of adult views about the role of media in children's recreational time is evident in the management of media play at this service. A conservative attitude towards video games, computers, and television, on one hand, and a love for movies, on the other hand, has resulted in a privileging of the feature film form. While this service offers children less in the way of video games and computer activities, its celebration of movies has resulted in a healthy production programme where children make movies.

Movie Magic: Making movies in OSHC

Since 2000, under the guidance and assistance of staff, children have completed production of one (video) movie each year in a programme they call, Movie Magic. The service has just completed (at the time of writing) its fourth production cycle and the programme generates double the normal OSHC attendance. Children who do not usually attend the service come along to participate in the movie-making project, and they bring their siblings. Among the six services in the larger study, this was the only one where children engaged in complex and prolonged media production. For the 2003 production, a fiction of recollection called *Déjà vu*, several historic places at quite a distance from the school site were used as shooting locations. In addition to their hours after school, the children were given a day off from school to participate in location shooting for the movie.

The first movie, completed in 1999, is a superhero fiction called *Cyberkid*. The second is called *Amelia Fry, Grade Five Spy* (2001), and several of the children say it is reminiscent of other films. The third movie, *Déjà vu* is a historical fiction about, as one child put it, 'this girl that got a chair and book from her grandpa and it's got all of her family history in it, like in photos. Every time she looks at it, she goes into that time and that place. And that's where all the scenes are.' The battle at Gallipoli and travel on the *Titanic*, in addition to scenes about lesser-known themes and events in Australian history, are among the many flashback sequences that connect the lead character to her family history and to world events. Each of the first three movies ran about 40 minutes in screen time, and the quality of technical and narrative execution has improved with each project.

The projects have also grown in their public recognition and appreciation with the 2003 screening attended by 400 people. The school has a student population of 500 and serves Reception (school entry at the age of five) through Grade Seven. Children who were not even in the movie came to the premiere with their families to see their friends in the movie. *Déjà vu* was the talk of this small town, a semi-rural, outer-urban community dominated by viticulture and the associated tourism industry. Community involvement in the projects has also grown over the years with the screenwriter of the film *Lantana*, a school parent, giving a script-writing workshop for the children during pre-production of *Déjà vu*. The school principal is so impressed with the programme that he is seeking to formalize ties between the recreational project and the school curriculum.

Movie Magic, now operating under the fictive production company title 'KidzBiz', grew out of a series of dramatic performance activities, and indeed the children's participation in the first films was mainly restricted to their performances.[2] Movie Magic is aimed at children in Grade Four and above but younger children participate in the movies by acting as extras in crowd scenes. As the programme has matured, the children's roles in production have expanded and they now take responsibility for a range of production tasks. The programme was initially developed as a strategy to retain the attendance at OSHC of children over the age of ten, or Grade Five, because funding for services was calculated on total attendance.

In 2000, the federal government replaced an operational subsidy to services with a funding scheme based on attendance. The new fee structure sets fees on a sliding scale, linked to household income. The fee for any individual child's attendance is based on the family's income. With these changes, OSHC services faced uncertain budgets and were urged to increase their overall attendance to reach an optimal minimum that would generate enough income to meet operational costs. Increasing overall attendance at the OSHC service was a critical need that drove the programme's development. If they could capture a greater attendance, their funding challenge might be met. (see Chapter 2 for more on funding.)

A secondary benefit of the programme has been an improvement in age and gender balance as more boys are continuing to attend the service to participate in the movie-making activities. Boys, more often than girls, cease to attend OSHC around the age of ten. This gender-based difference in attendance may have several explanations but since it has not been the focus of my study I can only offer speculative comment. Around the age of ten, boys may participate to a greater extent than girls

in other extra-curricular activities; they may be granted greater independence to return home from school alone; they may no longer find
OSHC programming engaging.

Consumer practices in the service of media education

Several years have passed since the first Movie Magic project began, and
the children now take responsibility for crew duties on their movie productions. Initially I was critical of the programme because I thought that
an unnecessary limitation had been placed on children's participation in
the projects. I wanted to write about a group of children making movies.
To me this meant children writing scripts, taking key production roles,
operating camera, making editing decisions, and having, what could be
called, 'creative control.' Although I still hold these ambitions, I now view
the Movie Magic model as an appropriate and particularly interesting production strategy for the way it articulates with the overall philosophy of
OSHC services in South Australia. Approaching movies from the fan's
point of view makes sense in this context because OSHC is a recreational
environment and movie going, for most people, is a recreational activity.
Movie Magic capitalizes on children's everyday consumer practices around
movies and audience experiences. The marketing–consumer nexus serves
as a welcoming entry-point to production.

I characterize the Movie Magic approach as Hollywood-like because
the programme embraces the commercial and populist notions of
audience and is replete with all the ancillary aspects of promotion and
marketing. Enjoyment of the product does not get lost in the process.
Movie Magic embraces the everyday pleasures of movie culture and does
not approach popular media as harmful or threatening to children or
childhood. Unlike classroom-based media education projects, that
might engage production as a form of critical analysis through exercises
in short-format video journalism in the vein of an electronic newsletter,
the end goal of Movie Magic has been a short feature of narrative fiction –
a movie for all intents and purposes.

Public debut of Movie Magic features have been presented in the
atmosphere of a gala premiere, down to the details of the red carpet, VIP
passes for performers and their guests, and paparazzi (children performing as rogue photographers). Marketing materials include colour posters
and each child gets to take home a copy of the movie (including cover
art), as if it were a title from the video shop. All of the practices surrounding the product emulate common consumer, fan, and industry
practices. Movie Magic is a scale model of a consumer's view of 'the

entertainment industry.' This approach to media production suits the nature of OSHC, offering child-centred recreational activities. It is also squarely placed in what David Buckingham has identified as a paradigm shift in media education. Movie Magic begins with what children '*already* know, and with their existing tastes and pleasures in the media, rather than assuming that these are merely invalid or "ideological"' (2003: 14).

Movie Magic's emphasis is on entertainment, and the learning that goes on around the movie-making process has been informal. No attention has been given to measuring retention of new skills or knowledge, although the children have acquired both. There is little in the Movie Magic concept, process, or product that resembles the type of media criticism so common to media education curricula. Movie Magic is positioned as a creative activity, like art making or cooking. Despite a lack of explicit curriculum goals and assessment, teachers and the school principal recognize Movie Magic as offering valuable learning opportunities to children. Due to the growth and success of the programme, the principal contributed use of an iMac computer and a digital video camera for the 2004 production cycle and has praised the programme publicly at their last screening event. Movie Magic has 'buy-in' from the school's administration. The OSHC Service Director says that the children

> improve their skills from year to year and that they demonstrate this development with 'increased confidence and commitment, team work across ages and friendships, following directions and instructions' and in their ability to talk about films. I would add that the staff have also learned from their experiences and honed their skills at assisting the children with each project.

As previously noted, I was initially critical of the programme's limitations. Having participated in the process, I was able to see that Movie Magic makes a valuable contribution to children's growing media competency by allowing them an opportunity to mobilize their fan and consumer knowledge in production activities. The programme and its process demonstrate how entertainment can serve as a scaffold for media education. In the following pages I outline and describe how Movie Magic intersects with key characteristics of industry and fan practices. By connecting with children's fan and consumer knowledge, Movie Magic situates production in terms that are already known to children, even if that knowledge is implicit. In making these connections, their tacit knowledge of consumption provides a firm base upon which children build new competencies in production. As they move through the processes of production, implicit knowledge becomes more explicit as they reflect on how and why their productions take a particular shape. Process and product, like production and consumption, are not neatly separable in creative activities.

Star power in kid production

Star power is an important aspect of popular film culture that the Movie Magic features have connected with. So far, all the movies have had a strong lead character and the child who wins this role is effectively 'the star.' Emily (Grade Eight) had the lead role in *Amelia Fry, Grade Five Spy*: 'We had to audition for whatever part we wanted and I wanted that part. Most of the girls wanted it, like a couple of my best friends. At least seven of us wanted it. They all got best friend roles.' When speaking with me, Emily was very clear about her interest in the next movie: 'I'd prefer to be in front of the camera than behind the scenes. I think I like the attention.'

Amber (Grade Seven) acted in *Déjà vu*: 'Me and my friends are definitely going to be in the next one [2004]. I don't really know what it's about but I'm going to try out for the main part.' When I asked Amber if she'd like to have responsibilities other than acting, she replied, 'I like performing and acting. I'm not very organized so I couldn't really be a technician. I'm not really good with computers. I'd love to write a script or write the story line.'

Amber's comments suggest several issues for closer examination but first let's take up her preference for acting. Before the first pre-production session in 2004, the Service Director held a meeting to assess interest in the programme so that he could establish a time line and have some estimation of how many children would be involved. Among the 45 children who showed up at a lunchtime meeting, only a couple of them wanted crew positions. *Most of the children wanted to be in the movie.* Earlier, when I asked a group of eight children who had been involved with previous productions if any of them would like to operate the camera in the next movie, only one child said yes. The rest wanted to act and reasoned that they could not be both behind the camera and on camera at the same time. Just like the stereotype of the aspiring Hollywood actor, they all wanted more screen time in the upcoming movie than they had in the previous production and those who were 'extras' before now want 'more lines.'

The children's preference for performance is not surprising when we consider that most people, adults included, have more knowledge of movie stars and actors than they do of any other aspect of feature film form or production roles. Movie stars are often the most accessible of on-screen elements in a film, even though actors would usually constitute the minority of workers on a production. Stars sell movies. We feel that we know about performance and performers because we watch movies and we pay attention to press coverage that promotes the stars and markets the movies. This point is made even more sharply in children's media as the collectible figures based on movie characters are among the most important elements of the extended narrative and marketing network (Kinder, 1991). Children also have more generic experience with performance, through make-believe and other forms of play, than they do for scripting, camera operation, editing, or any other aspect of movie production. It is not surprising then that initially they would be inclined to participate in a way that is familiar to them and, moreover, generates a certain public recognition. While acting may seem to restrict participation to one area of production, the children do learn about production through their participation in performance. The time that the first actors spent on set now informs their activities in crew capacities.

Genre and popular film culture

The Movie Magic programme also draws heavily upon children's knowledge of genre and their repertoire of popular film culture. During the script development stage for *Déjà vu*, according to the Service Director who takes responsibility for Movie Magic, many children expressed interest in the action genre and wanted to make a movie with special effects. *Déjà vu*, through the narrative convention of reminiscence, allowed for several genres to be referenced in numerous flashback sequences, including action. As the group was finalizing the script, a maritime museum was displaying a replica of a ship from the same period as the *Titanic*. The museum allowed the Movie Magic group to use the display as a set for location shooting. The script incorporated *Titanic* the ship and *Titanic* the international blockbuster to create one of the historic sequences that required special effects. As the lead character reads through the photo-scrapbook left to her by her grandfather, she discovers that she had a relative on the ship *Titanic*. The flashback sequence is triggered as she looks over the scrapbook and imagines her relatives on the sinking ship, even though she can only know them through the news clippings and other memorabilia left to her by her deceased grandfather. In an over-the-shoulder shot of a photo in the album, the image morphs into sepia tones for a transition to the romance and tragedy of *Titanic*'s fateful night. *Déjà vu* also sources the action of war movies in its recreation of the battle at Gallipoli and simultaneously the famous Australian film *Gallipoli*. It is important that these scenes evoke the well-known and popular films about these historic events, and not obscure documentaries.

When I asked the children if the movies they had made were like other movies, many of them told me that *Déjà vu* was like *Titanic* and that there are a lot of war films. Despite the pastiche practice that *Déjà vu's* story relies upon, the children did not discuss their movies in reference to other films unless I actively took this line of questioning. Emily initially rejected the idea that *Amelia Fry* was like other films: 'You can kind of tell it's just a little home made thing. I haven't seen any movies like it.' Her remarks first commented on the aesthetics and production values of *Amelia Fry*. On second thought, she noted that the story was similar to another film: 'Oh, it's kinda' like, it reminds me of the movie *Agent Cody Banks*,' she said and then quickly qualified the remark. 'It's just that Cody Banks is a school kid, he's 13 and becomes a spy and has lots of missions,' Emily said. Mike (Grade Six) also thought *Amelia Fry* was like another film, 'There's a video like *Amelia Fry*. It's about a girl spy that went to school. I think that's where he [Service Director] got the idea.' Several of the children commented on the poor quality of the sound in their movies and this was often the only difference they noted between their product and a Hollywood movie. The children like to see their movies as distinguished, but still within the system. They want to make the kind of movies they see in the theatre and hire from the shop. Attending to this desire is one way that Movie Magic sustains children's interest in the production process. By envisioning a product that is familiar, children see the process through with enthusiasm.

Talk about movies

In the pre-production, production, and consumption of their work, the children are encouraged to understand their movie projects and associated processes with reference to popular film culture. In dramatic performance workshops, production exercises, and story idea sessions, blockbuster movies and well-known Australian films are most often used to explain concepts and techniques. In a performance workshop I observed, all but one of the examples used to explain terminology were taken from blockbuster movies. In discussing improvisation, for example, the Service Director described a scene from *Pretty Woman* and explained that a particular exchange between the two lead characters was not in the script but had developed when Richard Gere added his own interpretive action during filming. Similarly, when explaining the importance of maintaining continuity, the children were given three examples of continuity errors from the films *Gladiator*, *Lord of the Rings*, and *Star Wars*. Most of the children knew these films and many knew the particular scenes by heart. This discussion quickly rose to a fever pitch as children eagerly added examples of other films with glaring continuity errors.

In a story idea session for the current productions, the children were asked, 'What would you like to see in our movie? What would you like our movie to be about?' They replied with a mix of references to genres, high concepts, and film titles. Children raised their hands and put forth their ideas. Among the genres were 'comedy,' 'real action movie,' and an 'old movie, set in the past.' Other suggestions included shorthanded remarks like 'exhilarating' and 'bullies.' One child said, 'I think it needs monsters' and another proposed a movie 'like *Cyberkid.*' This suggestion, that they re-make or produce a sequel to a previous Movie Magic production, generated almost unanimous endorsement from the rest of the children. In addition to testifying to the success of *Cyberkid*, it also demonstrates that the children situate their productions squarely within the context of the well-known commercial cinema.

At the third mention of *Tomb Raider*, the Service Director tried to shift the focus by telling the children, 'We don't want to just list all our favourite films because they've already been made.' The children, however, could not be dissuaded. The rest of the session revealed their screening histories and preferences through their suggestions to make movies like *Speed*, *Legally Blonde*, and *Matrix*. As they each made suggestions, the cumulative list eventually included something haunted, horror, sword fights and stuff like that, guns, BG – blood and guts – haunted, medieval, a band, Dracula, set in a different universe, ugliness, evil Doctors, and a tear-jerker. One child asked with great urgency, 'My pencil idea, did you put that down?' The Service Director responded that this idea could be incorporated into a scene but wasn't an idea for an entire movie. A few of the suggestions were not obviously linked to popular film, and among them was the idea for a story about a person who spoke in a completely different language that nobody understood.

Since interest among the children has grown, in 2004 the group was split into two production teams and each made a short movie (that is, shorter than the 45 minutes of previous projects). To incorporate several ideas into one script, they once again used the flashback device. *Dreamy Dion* (2005) is about a boy who daydreams. Many of the children's preferences and suggestions come to the screen in the lead character's vivid musings. Dion imagines himself as the star of a rock band, a famous artist at his own gallery show, fighting off clone bullies at school, and having his science project generate a Frankenstein-like monster.

The other movie, *Gob-smacked* (2005), takes up the idea of speaking a language that nobody else understands. A young girl so frustrates her grandmother by speaking in slang that the grandmother plots a sort of revenge scheme. When she sends the girl on a series of errands, each shopkeeper responds to the child's request by speaking in a language that she does not understand but without revealing any concern at the child's confusion. Among the languages are an Aboriginal pigeon, Italian, Cockney rhyming slang, and pig Latin. Utilizing local shops, the script incorporates the children's fondness for location shooting. The shopkeepers and patrons that the lead character encounters on her errands are played by the children in costume while the sets are provided by real locations (butcher shop, hairdresser, post office, etc.). Two or three location scenes were shot in each of several excursions to the town centre. As the cast and crew (cameraperson and assistant) for the particular scene took part in the shooting, the cast for the next scene waited outside and practiced their lines in between chatting and socializing. The children appeared to enjoy standing outside the shops in costume and waiving to the passing traffic as much as they did the actual production activities. The movies were completed in early 2005 and screened in a large hall with over 450 people in attendance.

Special effects and movie spectacle

The scripts have built on the children's expressed interest in special effects and movie spectacle. The storylines constructed with a heavy emphasis on flashback allow the children to experiment with production techniques, like blue screen, and post-effects like the sepia tint. Looking closely at the children's dialogue around movie pre-production, one can see how they work across the consumption–production divide and integrate one with the other. Their comments indicate how much they know about movies and how they apply this knowledge to their own productions. A few examples from the second pre-production workshop in 2004 demonstrate this process.

In the explanation and discussion of framing, composition, and focal length, the Service Director used examples from previous Movie Magic productions. He explained to the group,

> You know cameras have a zoom. You can zoom in and get closer. Remember when we made our first movie, we used the zoom a lot, and it really didn't look that good. We learned that it's better to use two different shots and edit them together. Next time you're watching a movie, look at how many shots there are in a scene and how they are different.

Following this explanation, a scene was defined as a set of actions and a series of shots occurring in a particular location. Jade then added, 'On a DVD you can select scenes and skip some and do things like that.' With this remark, Jade is integrating what she already knows about scenes, that they are units in a DVD, with what she has just learned about scenes. The discussions around production techniques encourage children to associate knowledge from different experiences and contexts with the task at hand, planning a production of their own.

After listening to an explanation of terminology associated with camera work ('close-up,' 'medium shot,' 'wide shot,' and so forth), the children eagerly asked questions about cinematography. With even the first question the children were expanding on what they had been introduced to. Edward asked, 'How do you do bird's-eye view in a movie?' They are told about crane shots and cameras mounted on airplanes and a range of techniques for achieving such a shot. Harry then asks, 'How would we do that? Hire a cherry picker?' The session continued like this, with one child asking a question about a shot in a popular film and another child asking a follow-up question about how the Movie Magic crew might emulate the effect or style.

Adam asked, 'Say you want to get a shot of something moving really fast and you don't want to get the blurry lines, how would you do that? How would you get them both perfect?' David offered up the idea of a tracking shot, 'where the camera is mounted on tracks.' And another child added, 'Like at the [horse] races!' And yet another child contributed his observations from the recent Clipsal 500 V-8 auto race.

Not only the content but also the manner in which the discussion proceeded is interesting. The children shared knowledge from personal observation (i.e. at the races), research (David has a book on special effects and cites it often), viewing practices (i.e. what's included in the DVD extras), and even visits to theme parks, like Warner Bros. Movie World.

They alternated interrogation with exemplification, and asked questions of one another and of the adults present (myself and the Service Director). Because each child could claim knowledge and expertise from their fan practices, they were all able to contribute to the discussion.[3]

Within the context provided by the shared production project, they exchange information drawn from a range of experiences and sources and build their collective knowledge of movies and movie-making. In preparing to make a movie, the Movie Magic children demonstrate the process of scaffolding knowledge as individuals and as a collective. Their consumer practices are validated and made relevant to the production and the group discussions help build their understanding of how movies work. Although the workshops demystify the movies, the magic remains.

More important than its status as a method of curriculum design, scaffolding is fundamentally a way of thinking. Scaffolding knowledge is what the learner does when drawing upon prior knowledge, intuition, preferences, and everyday experiences. While the first pre-production workshop in 2004 mined the children's knowledge of Hollywood movies, genres, and storylines, the second workshop embraced their collective production experience in addition to their knowledge of consumer practices. Movie Magic invites children to draw upon their consumer experiences and apply that body of knowledge in production activities.

Take two: Room for improvement

Given the resources from which this programme operates, limited equipment, limited staffing, and time constraints, the projects that they have achieved and the increasing sophistication and continual improvement in execution from project to project are commendable. There is, however, room for improvement. The programme seems to exist as a trade for the absence of other media (television and video games). The movie-making projects are, despite the benefits I have outlined, still driven by adults rather than children. Children's participation in the technical crew positions and responsibilities could be improved by giving them more responsibility and opportunity. (This would necessarily prolong the production process.)

It is particularly troubling that girls, more often than boys, attributed to themselves technical incompetence or expressed a lack of confidence in their technical abilities, as Amber's comments illustrated ('I'm not very organized so I couldn't really be a technician.'). Girls did not demonstrate less technical ability than boys did but girls willingly shared with me their insecurities about technical skills and tasks in a way that boys did not. Perhaps the boys also have these insecurities and simply did not share them with me. This may be an aspect of gender performance in which girls feel free to express 'techno phobia' without social penalty. It may also have been a pragmatic decision. Since all the children understood that they could not be on camera and behind camera at the same time, opting out of crew responsibilities may have been a strategy to ensure an acting role in the movie. Some children may have thought that in addition to simply wanting to act, their case for a performance role would be strengthened by a declared inability to take up a crew position. I am not suggesting that Movie Magic is responsible for the views these girls expressed but rather that Movie Magic and OSHC provide opportunities for children to succeed in activities that are new to them or which have not been their usual realm for success. Movie Magic might be an activity through which some girls find out that they are technically capable.

The girls who did take on technical tasks were just as capable as the boys who took on technical roles, and the director did see to it that one boy and one girl were active in camera operation for each production. Although it is beyond the scope of this research to determine why girls are not very eager to take up crew positions, it is important to consider how all children might be more encouraged in this direction. As a first step towards greater inclusion of girls in the technical roles, staff could organize production exercises so that each child has to take up each technical position in rotation. Rather than drawing attention to gender, requiring all children to attempt each position achieves female inclusion without explicitly marking it (Fusco).

Changing the emphasis from technology to aesthetics may also have an effect on children's interest in crew positions. For instance, talking about camera operation in terms of framing and composition instead of hardware and technology may change the way children perceive cameras and camera operation. Those who understand camera operation as a technical skill and feel intimidated by technology might be more inclined to take up the challenge of camera operation if it were presented as an artistic endeavour rather than a technical skill (Buckingham, Grahame, and Sefton-Green, 1995). As photographers are quick to point out, it is not the camera that takes the picture but the photographer. The phrase 'to have a photographer's eye' suggests the aesthetic and perceptual dimensions of the craft and art that would be completely missed if the expression were 'to have a photographer's camera.'

Movie Magic could also take greater input from children in the scripting process, as Amber and other children suggested. While the ideas for the 2004 storylines came from the children, the actual scripts and story-boards were created by the adult staff member. With *Gob-smacked*, once the story idea was selected, the children were broken into small groups and asked to generate some dialogue and come up with some crazy kid-speak for the lead character. This session rapidly lost focus and the children did not achieve much useful dialogue because they did not have firm parameters within which to create this dialogue. The scenes had not yet been set, the locations were not secured, and the children were asked to write dialogue without enough knowledge of the plot. In retrospect, a better plan for inclusion of children in the scripting process would be to continue with the story idea sessions by having the children shape a series of scenes and plot points before attempting to script any dialogue.

This strategy would increase the children's input in several ways. Given defined settings and a plot point, children could more easily generate dialogue and action for that scene. Once several scenes are scripted, transitions between them could be worked out in a process similar to the story idea sessions, where the group works together to put the bits in sequence. The script could then be broken down and returned to the children for storyboarding with small groups working on individual scenes. Expanding the children's input in this fashion may result in different kinds of stories. To date, the Movie Magic projects bear a certain mark of legitimacy; they are not transgressive or playful in the ways that many researchers have noted for youth productions. This may be the result of heavy influence by adults on the scripting process. Would their scripts be more edgy or challenging of social norms if the children had a greater role in authorship? Since little has been written about production by children in the OSHC age bracket (5–12), these are questions for further study.

Greater value also could have been derived from the story idea sessions by asking the children more about the films that they were suggesting as models for their own film. We can guess at what they meant when they suggested *Speed*, *Matrix*, and *Tomb Raider*, but since the opportunity to reflect on the appealing qualities of those films in greater detail was missed, we do not really know what about *Tomb Raider* they would want to build on in their own script. A three-step process could extend this exercise. One at a time, ask a child to summarize the story of a favourite movie. The adult(s) could then highlight elements of the narrative structure. Finally, a discussion of how the story is told in film form would expose the children to the nuts and bolts of the story/film relationship. This does require the adult(s) to have considerable knowledge of film but this seems a reasonable expectation if that is the programme on offer. Through the discussion, the children might be able to isolate features of their favourite films that they would like to emulate in future productions. More focussed activities like this discussion might generate more ideas like *Gob-smacked* while also adding to the educational component of the programme.

Implementing the type of reforms suggested above would add considerable time to the pre-production process and risk greater attrition from children on the project. It is the performing and shooting that the children love and prolonging the lead-up time to these activities may well result in fewer children actually seeing the project through. We ought to ask whether a recreational media project requires the kind of commitment that a classroom activity demands? Must we apply the same standards in OSHC that we would in other circumstances? If a child does not want to play out an entire ball game in OSHC, s/he does not have to. A child can leave a given activity at any time and take up something else. Should movie-making be any different? Perhaps a recreational media project should be understood more flexibly and children's participation in these projects could be more fluid, like other forms of play where children drop in and drop out as they choose. To maintain continuity, it is only the acting roles that require a long-term commitment. In terms of process, the children might gain equal benefit by being able to participate on a more ad hoc basis, even if this means a longer production cycle. It is difficult to predict whether this model would work but it is an option that could be trialed.

Another way to enhance media education while maintaining the recreational nature of media in OSHC would be to more closely align the recreational movie screenings with the Movie Magic productions. Movie selection for viewing could be more purposefully planned to link with the activities of Movie Magic. This could include post-screening, moderated discussions about the movies the children watch, with an emphasis on the features that the children have shown an interest in during Movie Magic sessions (for example, special effects, cinematography, action choreography, and so forth). Movies directed or produced by women could raise awareness of the contribution of women to film culture and, through this awareness, encourage girls to participate behind the camera.

Since little has been written about children's recreational media production, that is production outside the dominant 'media literacy' paradigm and outside classrooms, the opportunity to experiment with programme design and strategies is vast. Each recreational programme that offers media production will face a unique set of challenges based on the composition of their community and resources. The programming challenge for staff is to embrace the flexibility of recreational care and the pleasures of play when developing new strategies for children's media production. Production programmes should improve with each offering, and small changes should not be discouraged as the undertaking is a considerable one and changing an already complex programme is not easy.

Movie Magic not only offers a unique media education programme but it also builds relationships across the three domains of home, classroom, and OSHC. Movie Magic has proven to be a community-building venture and one that reinforces the connections between home, classrooms, and OSHC without dismissing their differences and unique qualities (Halpern, 2003: 116).

The considerable time and resources allocated to the movie-making projects are significant, and in light of the limitations that the management at this service has established for other media, it is interesting in other ways as well. The restrictions placed on video game play and the limited use of free-to-air television suggest that these media are not legitimate recreational activity for children. This contradiction does not seem to create conflict between the adults and children because children are used to such regulation being imposed by adults and they accept the rules as part of the OSHC experience, even if they would prefer it to be otherwise.

Movie Magic, for its limitations, is an exceptional example of media production, if a somewhat circumscribed example of informal learning. Indeed the adult direction and control that is exerted over the entire process undermines the critical tenet of informal learning in that the adult here acts as instructor. Although there is no obligation to a curriculum, the children do not have more agency than the adult in the overall execution of the project (Livingstone, 2006). The entire programme is predicated on the lofty goal of completing a 'movie,' as I have described with reference to seemingly commercial criteria. To achieve this goal, the programme requires the kind of instructor intervention that is noted here. There are certainly other models for media production and movie production in particular, but the community here is pleased with the process and products to date and it is not likely that they will acquire the additional resources to implement a different type of programme around movie-making.

Nevertheless the programme does provide several other characteristic experiences of informal learning. Capitalizing on the children's generic knowledge of entertainment media is quite different to what is undertaken in formal schooling settings. Engaging the children in the script development and in the production activities, although limited here, is still a positive experience. Since it is such a positive experience for children, it is hoped that given future opportunities they will be eager to engage in other media production.

OSHC services can implement other media production activities that are less resource demanding and which give children more agency. There is a vast range of activities that can be undertaken with computer software and mobile phones, for instance. Among the most accessible activities are some that promote critical reflection on a variety of other media play that is common to OSHC. For instance, children can be encouraged to produce 'zeens' about their video game, television, or movie cultures. With basic word processing and image-production tools they can produce a paper or electronic publication that delivers to its readership reviews of games, essays about games, examples of game art, cheats, and a range of other useful, entertaining, and critical information about games and game culture. Similar materials can be produced for public display in a large format on bulletin boards and as decorative enhancement to the OSHC environment.

Given the access and tools, children can create their own game characters for existing games or they can even write their own games for computers. Mobile phones can be an asset rather than a hindrance to the community if they are used to create digital media content that can be shared publicly. The simplest of mobile phone-assisted activities is to take photographs but there is a wide range of share-ware available to assist in more creative production of animations and text-based entertainment and communication.

Developing and promoting a digital media culture in an OSHC community is best supported by investing in staff development and training around these activities. The biggest shortfall in resources is staffing. OSHC services normally do not have staff who are knowledgeable or trained in media production. To shift the emphasis from media play to media production, the service must be willing and able to promote media production activities. Most services located on school grounds have the technical resources required for such activities in the school's computing provisions. What is lacking at OSHC is the know-how required to guide such activities and to recognize the possibility of programming around such projects because, on the whole, staff are not digitally savvy.

9
Practice and Play

Theory and practice in children's media play

The careful and in-depth examination of children's media use in Out of School Hours Care (OSHC) that informs this book has generated theoretical implications and a set of associated practical applications. Documentation and analysis of children's media use in after-school care services has shown that rather than being dictated by constraints of the medium or marketing, media use is significantly shaped by social factors. It can be said that children's media practices and habits are site specific because what they do at home, in the classroom, and at OSHC differs significantly. I have argued that these differences, which mark media use in after-school care, are the result of unique environmental and social circumstances that define after-school care as both a place and an experience.

In after-school care, children use media in a leisurely fashion, and leisure itself is constituted within a set of relations to time and space. I have described the experience of time and space in after-school care as an intermediary one. This is perhaps a convention that establishes yet another false set of boundaries but it is, for the time being, a useful distinction. Children's practices and habits with media in after-school care are informed by their practices elsewhere but are also significantly shaped by the time and space relations that are unique to after-school care rather than the media that are found there. Within the time/space experience of OSHC, children use media in particular ways that take advantage of the temporal, spatial, and social opportunities afforded by OSHC.

After-school care in Australia strives to be affectively like an ideal family home, which I have argued may not even exist. Nevertheless the ideal is a powerful one that dictates an orientation to leisure time and

165

the way leisure activities are constituted and constructed. Thus media use in after-school care is, where possible, open and only lightly managed at a micro-level by adults. At a macro-level, media regulation in OSHC takes guidance from systems of regulation that originate in the wider society like the OFLC classification scheme and the broadcast schedule, both of which suggest or impose certain restraints on media provision, access, and use. These regulatory systems are the same systems that 'regulate' household consumption of media, returning again to the ideal family home and ideas about the place of children after-school and the place of media in children's lives.

The intermediary nature of after-school care is notable in its configuration of media provision and the way these media are used by children in play. Unlike classrooms, the use of media in OSHC is playful. Unlike family homes, the use of media in OSHC is collaborative and social, almost always a group endeavour and rarely an individual pursuit. Time at play is also less structured than in classroom exercises but more constrained than family homes because resources are scarcer in OSHC. Demand for these resources, coupled with a fairness principle that would see every child have access, exerts limitations that are not always in effect in family homes. These features have, if not generated the practices we observed, allowed us to recognize practices and patterns of use that have not been noted for family homes or classrooms. Children's management of turn taking and sharing video game consoles is one such play pattern. The game of Playground Pokemon, where children physically enact imaginative play scenarios loosely based on the TV show and game characters, is an example of how limited access spurs creative expansion of media play in other arenas.

The recreational environment of OSHC also allows for structured media activities to be pursued in a fashion that might not find a place in the time and space experience of classrooms. The Movie Magic programme is an example of this. While Movie Magic is structured to deliver an outcome, a movie, the way that outcome is achieved is quite different to classroom activity in both execution and effect. The children were not assessed on their contributions, and the recognition of attaining the goal (the final public screening) was celebrated in a way that is not typical of schooling. On the night, it seemed as if all contributions had been equal; the films and their crews were celebrated as if each individual contribution were equal to all others because the films could not have been completed without the collaborative effort.

We have also seen how school resources are put to different purposes in OSHC, especially where computers are involved. Children use computers in OSHC for a wider variety of purposes than they do at home or at school. One could say that a greater potential of the computer is exploited at OSHC than either in classrooms or family homes. In addition, practices associated with classrooms and the home environment are enacted in OSHC but with variation that is characteristic of its unique time and space experience. Children work collaboratively on both recreational activities and school assignments in OSHC, while the 'time on task' can be more leisurely and committed or more furtive than in classrooms.

The research suggests that children's media practices and media play in OSHC provide important opportunities for informal learning around media and they contribute to children's ongoing acquisition of media competency. It would therefore seem appropriate that policy and planning take this into account. By seriously considering the provision of media technologies in recreational environments like OSHC, children's informal learning would be better supported and catered for.

Just as I was completing this book, I took a research trip to observe children's media use in Swedish after-school care services, what are called *fritids* (for children 6- to 9-years-old) and *öppen fritidsverksamhet* (for children 10- to12-years-old). Listening to research presentations at conferences over the past five years, I had the impression that media use in Swedish after-school care services was plentiful and unencumbered by suspicion and fear. I expected to find children playing video and computer games, engaging in digital production, and freely incorporating media play with other forms of play. I hoped to discover models of 'best practices' in media use and media play.

To my surprise, and disappointment, children's media play in *fritids* and *öppen fritidsverksamhet* has come under closer restriction recently. The concern over rising rates of childhood obesity has hit Sweden, and the position of media play in children's recreation is suffering as a result. According to *fritids* staff workers and directors, parents have been requesting that media play at *fritids* be limited because *children spend so much time playing with media at home*. Rather than limit use at home, parents are seeking restrictions in *fritids* and requesting more outdoor and physical play at *fritids*.

Such requests indicate that Swedish parents, like most adults, are not aware of the distinctions in media practices that are generated by differences in social setting. Assuming that parents do have their children's best interests at heart, it would seem that they are not aware of the benefits of media play in peer-group environments. While it is reasonable to monitor the total amount of time children spend with media to ensure that they engage in a range of activities, restriction of media use at home would seem the better option, given the generally high quality of media play at after-school care and the variable quality at home. Children's recreational media use in peer-group settings, like after-school care services, is by definition more social than their media use at home and the social dimensions of that play support their preferred play style and learning (see Figure 9.1).

Media use in OSHC is:

- Social & Collaborative

- Leisurely and Playful

- Creative

- Public

- Peer-regulated

- Restricted and limited due to resource pressures

- Related, but different, to home media use

- Related, but different, to classroom media use

Fundamental factors that shape media use in OSHC are:

- Media provision (hardware and software)

- Use of space (environment and location)

- Regulatory schemes (social practices and rules)

Goals for Media Use in OSHC include:

- Making media use more public

- Maintaining the emphasis on social use of media

- Using consumer media to encourage media production

- Linking consumption of entertainment media with other activities

Figure 9.1   Critical research findings about media use in after-school care

Popular notions about how children interact with media, what they do with media, and how media are situated in their lives have developed from two dominant research paradigms. One is the study of children in classrooms and the other is the study of children in family homes. The idea of media literacy emerged as a response to concern over the place and role of media in children's lives, and by moving media into classrooms, media education became formalized. The best place to secure a population of children for research of all sorts has been in classrooms. Media that are mainly experienced elsewhere, movie theatres or at home in the case of TV, have been studied in classrooms and laboratories (Luke, 1990: 65), and neither environment has been the 'natural' home of media.

The important work that has been done around media in the domestic sphere has also shaped our perspective on children's media practices, and restricted that view. Television rapidly became a medium to be experienced in the family home, rather than in public gathering spots, not because the content or the technology was best suited to this form of consumption but because manufacturers would sell more TV sets if they were placed in individual households instead of public gathering places. Between our scrutiny of children in family homes and classrooms, we overlooked the other places where children and media converge.

The 'digital revolution' has brought significant reconsideration of many assumptions in media research. The notion of 'interactivity' has gained prominence in marketing campaigns and in our understanding of what it means to use media. Simultaneously we have seen a trend towards miniaturization and mobility as key features of media technologies. These developments have given researchers pause to consider the collaborative nature of media use and the significance of place in popular media cultures. It should not be surprising that we are unaware of the unique benefits of media play in after-school care because there has been such little attention paid to this area of children's lives and to the influence that these settings have on media cultures.

With increased adult participation in the workforce and growing fears about children's safety, supervised OSHC services and programmes are rapidly becoming the after-school place of choice for more children. Given the benefits of recreational and social media use, the pleasures children experience through media play, and the ever-increasing importance of media in our everyday lives, it is only reasonable that we seek to find acceptable ways of incorporating media play in after-school care environments.

The benefits of public recreational media access

Australian children are lucky. Here the dominant view is that children's after-school time is leisure time. In the US, it seems that leisure time is available to fewer and fewer children. If a child performs poorly in school, recreation time rapidly becomes remediation time. For high achievers, after-school time is often spent on academic enrichment activities designed to ensure a fast track to university and future employment. Children's playtime is indeed becoming very precious. This passage from 'Linking and Learning,' a recently issued report from the US Department of Health and Human Services (2006), summarizes trend in the US:

> Afterschool programs can also benefit by measuring their effective-ness in terms of educational outcomes. Many programs already pro-vide homework help, tutoring services, and/or remedial education activities, while others seek to improve attitudes toward education and learning by allowing youth to explore new areas that comple-ment the school day. The 2002 No Child Left Behind (NCLB) law opened the door for extending learning into the afterschool hours by strengthening the academic components of the 21st Century Community Learning Center Program (21CCLC).
>
> (p. 20)

Recent research on children's media use at home tells us that although parents are interested in knowing what their children do online, they are often unaware of the details of their children's Internet use at home. Many parents believe that their children are doing schoolwork on the family computer, but children report that during this time they are often using communication applications to 'chat' with friends via the Internet (ABA, 2005). Only a portion of children's online time at home is spent doing the homework that their parents think they are doing. Not much has changed since the early 1990s when research showed that children most often used the home computer to play games when parents thought they were studying (Giacquinta, Bauer, and Levin, 1993). Parents' estimations and children's reports of how much time children are giving to social Internet use (rather than school use) are inconsistent with one another. Parents underestimate how much time children give to Internet chat rooms, email, instant mes-saging, and similar communication functions supported by social net-working sites on the Internet. Rather than stir panic, these findings should demonstrate how difficult it is for even the best-intentioned adults to oversee children's media use.

The explosion of new media in family homes means that parents now have additional responsibilities for provision, supervision, and management of a wider array of media, some of which may not interest them. At the same time, parents may be reluctant to assert their supervisory authority, as requests to limit media use in after-school care would suggest. The data in the ABA study on children's Internet use suggest the importance of media access for children in public and supervised spaces. Most importantly, the provision of entertainment and educational media in public spaces is still, for some children, the only access that they have.

Many people might think that schools provide children with access to important media and the education to make good use of these tools. Indeed, while children's media use is supervised and regulated in classrooms, it is limited and adult directed in the main. Although some children may spend endless hours playing unsupervised with media at home, in classrooms it is just the opposite. Lessons often do not allow for leisurely contemplation and revision. In OSHC, when resources are sufficient, media use can be approached by children in a leisurely fashion. Like all the other activities on offer, media use is supported as recreation and for the value that it adds to children's leisure pursuits. But, recreational media use has the benefit of informing other uses of media. Intermediary spaces like OSHC effectively bring together the media that we find in living rooms and classrooms, allowing children create links between the two spaces and across media as they develop their media competency.

At the outset of this book I argued that banning children from media does not help them become responsible consumers or participants in media exchange. The recreational use of media in OSHC allows children to learn and practice self-management as media consumers because children are given a degree of autonomy over their own choices and activities. With their peers, children make their own decisions about how media are used in OSHC. Many of the media activities that children enjoy in their leisure share features with the more formal and serious uses of media that constitute twenty-first-century literacy. Conducting database research employs skills similar to those used when looking up football scores on the Web. Building and managing a virtual city calls upon generic strategy and planning skills. Writing about video games and for video games engages the writer in analytical and creative thinking and expression. OSHC is well positioned to support the links between recreational media use and enduring, transferable skills.

Ensuring equity and building competency in play

OSHC services give children important access to media. For many children, OSHC is the only recreational access point they have for a range of media. In order for children to develop their media competency across the range of educational and social dimensions that communication technologies now serve, OSHC provides a critical service. Assuring recreational access to media for children, who would otherwise be socially marginalized by their lack of access or experience, is a valuable contribution that OSHC makes to children's lives. Over time, with the tendency of market penetration to result in lower consumer pricing of new technologies, these technologies become more affordable for home use. Despite the importance of these media in children's culture, children's ownership and control over communication and entertainment media in the home is often circumscribed by parental desires, needs, abilities, values, and practices. Children can become second-class consumers where media are involved.

For the 20 to 25 per cent of children who do not have home computers and software compatible with those used in school, OSHC can provide important extended time for social and educational use of computers. One of the defining characteristics of play is that it is often self-regulated and peer regulated, rather than directed by external authority. In OSHC, although media use is shaped and restricted by external variables like availability, children are relatively self-directed and self-monitoring in their use of media, albeit within the limits of what is provided. As individuals within peer groups they negotiate the use of media as play. I explained in Chapters 3, 4, 6, and 7 several ways in which children's play with media in OSHC differs from their media use in classrooms and family homes.

There are two key findings to highlight with respect to equity. First is that access to the school's computer network should be a goal for all services on school sites. There is no substitute. Children who want to work on school assignments or to apply what they have learned to a recreational pursuit of their own design will do this if they are given the tools. Secondly, similar to the findings of many other studies, the girls that we observed were not as inspired by video games as their male peers appeared to be. Interviews with the girls did not give us enough data to state assuredly that video games were perceived by them as masculine or that boys had colonized the game play in OSHC. Girls more often reported that they did not sign up early enough to get a turn and that eventually they stopped trying. Indeed, video game play was a large group activity in most services and the majority of players were often boys. If, as earlier research has shown, girls prefer to play video games with one or two players and not in a large and noisy group setting, then the atmosphere around video games in OSHC services may not be supporting girls' *preferences in play* (Vered, 1998b). Based on what girls told this research team, the game selection was also limited and not always to their liking. On the other hand, computers were appealing to girls and they used computers at OSHC as frequently as boys did. Gender equity is thus another reason to seek access to the school's computer network and provide computer stations in OSHC.

With respect to equity in access, it is not enough to have hardware and software on site. The software selection must reflect a wide range of tastes and the hardware must be made available to all the children. This requires considerable effort on the part of management. In addition to offering more than one station for video game play, software selection should be calculated and deliberate. Taking suggestions from children often results in hearing from only the keenest enthusiasts. Soliciting suggestions for software from the children who less frequently make use of the hardware may result in a very different mix, of both software and players. OSHC staff can also consult with retail sales outlets to find out what software titles girls are interested in. Turn taking and access to hardware is something that adults need to monitor so that all the children feel they have a chance to access the gear and play games of their choice.

Managing media play in OSHC

Media play in OSHC is but one option among many. A fundamental operating philosophy of OSHC services is to provide a range of recreational activities suited to children's needs and abilities. This goal is met through programmes that offer a balance of indoor and outdoor, restful and energizing activities, some attending to long-term and others to short-term attention and so forth. Media play can be suited to all of these criteria but how can adults ensure that children are individually engaging across the range of activities? Providing diversions that appeal to the range of tastes represented in a large group is different from catering to the individual needs of any individual child in a single day. Many adults believe that children's play should be diversified at individual levels; that within one day a child should engage across a range of activities. In this respect, media play is most often considered an activity that should be moderated: children should play with media in moderation so that other activities such as art and sport can be part of their leisure-time fare.

Media play poses a certain contradiction as play because one of the defining characteristics of play is that it is not structured by rigid external timetables. Effectively, play is for school-aged children what leisure is for adults; play is experienced as unstructured time. OSHC services can circumvent this contradiction, and placate parental concern over how much time children spend with media, by having limited media resources. The scarcity of resources in television monitors, video games machines, and the like enforces moderation. During the course of our observations, the most restricted medium was the computer. Only one service met the children's demand for access to computers and this was achieved by utilizing the school's computer room almost daily. None of the children at this service expressed a need or desire for more computer time and they demonstrated the widest range of computer use across the 'work'–leisure divide. At other services, however, children told us that they would like more opportunities to use the computers for both school work and recreational pursuits. Some children also criticized the software for both computers and video games. Most criticism of video games selection came from girls who found the selection unappealing. At some services, the older children were critical of the software selection for computers because they viewed the games as juvenile and thought the selection was too small.

Media access

A combination of scarce resources and high demand for media in OSHC, more than any other factors, have shaped the management of media play. The systems of turn taking and group play with video games that I described in Chapter 4 are generated, largely, by the high demand that children put on one video game machine (in services with more than 20 children per day). Children developed sophisticated turn-taking systems while playing in groups as a response to popularity of video games. A vast majority of children said that they preferred playing video games with companions and often did not have this option at home, where nearly 50 per cent said they played alone. OSHC was, for many children, the only place where they played video games with peers.

This, coupled with the common parental view that children should use entertainment media in moderation, is a reasonable argument for maintaining a limit on the hardware provision for video games. As I explained in previous chapters, most services have only one video game set-up. While this limitation does help structure access, it is in some cases, too limiting.

In the services that provided two video game machines and adequate playing spaces, children were able to segregate themselves by taste and age so that different software could be used on the two machines simultaneously. In these services, older children were able to play video games that appealed to their tastes while younger children were able to play with other games, elsewhere. Parents of younger children may find this beneficial because younger children have the option to stay with their peer group if they wish. OSHC staff may also enforce segregation around content if they have the hardware to support such a division. Without two machines, however, it is likely that younger children will play with older ones, and if there is a concern around content, the software selection would fall to the lowest common denominator: software that appeals to younger children. Eventually, this means that older children are likely to abandon this activity in favour of others.

Having two video game machines also allows services to offer segregated play so that different taste cultures can be catered for simultaneously and consistently. Older and younger children or boys and girls, as collectives, can have their own tastes represented among the options. As previous research has shown and interviews with girls in this study confirm, in public space with scarce resources boys tend to set the social tone around video and computer game play and it often offends the sensibilities of girls. Girls will opt not to play when they feel the social space has been colonized by masculinity (Vered, 1998b). Girls' taste in game software is also influenced by the public nature of game playing. Many girls play violent and competitive games in the privacy of their own homes, but are less inclined to play these games in public with boys. To provide software and playing opportunities that appeal to girls, it is helpful to have the resources that will support their preferences in play. Although it is possible to alternate use of resources on particular days, for instance Mondays and Wednesdays are 'girls only' days, such alternation runs the risk of excluding the children who come only on Tuesdays and Thursdays. To best resource video game play, services might aim to provide two machines and place them at a distance from one another, effectively establishing two gaming zones. This way, segregation by age, gender, or any other construct can be facilitated with a wider selection of software.

The spatial arrangements at one service also concerned the research team because the computers were secluded in a small storage room. Each of the five computers in this space would often be attended by a boy, and it was rare to see girls in this space. Although the placement of these computers had to do with space restrictions and security for the hardware, effectively it created a 'boys' club' where girls did not participate. In a situation like this one, if the computers could not be moved to create two different computer use spaces, experimenting with a system of alternation between boys and girls might be useful. If, given a 'girls only' day, girls did utilize the space and equipment, it might be productive to implement a temporary system of gender-segregated play to establish a girl presence in the space. After some time, eliminating the segregated play would show whether or not girls and boys would play together once an even footing was established.

More than consumption: Media production as play

In Chapter 8, Movie Magic, a programme that engages children in video movie production from script to screen was described. It was the only supervised production endeavour we encountered but its success indicates that extended production activities with other media would provide appealing recreational activities.

Since computer use was popular with all the children, younger and older, boys and girls, socially gregarious and shy alike, a range of production activities could be undertaken in this medium to great success. During the study none of the services took advantage of their access to computers to drive any creative production activities. While art and craft projects that were designed, provisioned, and supervised by adults were standard fare among all the services, these activities were restricted to traditional materials using sculptural, drawing, painting, ceramic, and collage techniques. Projects that utilize paper and paints, glitter and glue, feathers and fur can easily be transferred to the electronic domain and realized electronically. Engaging in more programming and creative media projects also satisfies the demand that children's media play be productive play, as I explained in Chapter 5.

Children consistently used computers for drawing and design activities of their own volition, and it is clear that electronic 'craft' (production) builds on activities that children already practice in both the analogue and digital realms. There is a wide range of free and bundled software available for PC that supports digital creativity like 'Photostory' (to manage and display digital photographs, including audio accompaniment),

'Movie Maker' (a digital editing tool for audio and video), and 'Audacity' (a sound recording and editing package). Simple animations can be made with 'Powerpoint,' and 'KidPix' offers a range of creative uses. 'Squeak' is an open-source, free, media-authoring tool developed by researchers interested in helping children learn with computers (www.squeak.org). 'Squeak' can be used to realize a wide variety of goals and projects.

In addition to providing the technical resources, extending media production in OSHC also requires that adults view media production as a 'useful activity' or legitimate leisure. Moreover, OSHC services must make staff development around digital media a priority. Staff need to feel more comfortable with media tools if they are to guide children in media production, as they do with more traditional recreational activities such as cooking, craft, and sport.

In addition to making media, OSHC also provides an interesting place for children to comment on their consumption and production of media. Since most services show movies at least once a week, a movie board is an easy way to foster a critical media culture by reflecting on consumer practices. Children can write movie reviews, draw the characters and create their own, write treatments for sequels, and engage in other creative activities around movie criticism. These projects can be displayed alongside movie classification information and a screening schedule. The publicly posted information on screenings and classifications (that is, G, PG, and so on) helps children become well-informed consumers and demonstrates to parents that media use in OSHC is not an electronic babysitter but is instead part of the wider set of leisure practices that enhance media competency. These materials can be produced for online circulation at very little cost.

In Chapter 4, I described how children take their video game play and extend it into live action, physical activity on the playground. Children repurpose material from one medium to another and from the virtual to the lived experience. With material that they are keenly interested in, children can develop and extend play into other domains. This is essentially media production. If the children who played 'Pokemon on the Playground' had been given access to computers, they might have started to write their own games. 'Game Maker,' a programme for developing games, is available online for 15 Euros and a less complex version is available as freeware.

As hardware and software standards change so rapidly, it is impossible to provide a list of resources that will remain relevant and accessible for the life of this book. The online Human-Computer Interaction (HCI) Bibliography provides a section on 'Kids and Computers' in association with the list CHI-Kids (http://www.hcibib.org/kids). CHI-Kids is a special interest group within the ACM (Association for Computing Machinery), the leading association for computing research and practice. The focus of CHI-Kids is discussion 'related to the creation and implementation of kids' media and technology' (http://sigchi.org/kids/chi-kids.html). In addition to the online bibliography and archived discussions, requests for information and recommendations can be posted to the list.

Portable stereo systems at several services provided the background rhythms for girls' choreography. They would spend hours organizing dance routines and one another. Building media production into their activity, the routines could easily be videotaped by other children using a consumer-quality, digital video camera and edited using the school's computers. A new dance video could be produced and screened each term.

When we conducted our research, social networking sites on the Internet were just emerging and were not yet the significant pillar of children's media culture that they have recently become. Similarly, mobile phones were only just emerging as part of the standard suite of school bag contents. When they did appear, they were widely restricted in classrooms and after-school care services. With recent developments in both these arenas, social networking sites and mobile phones demonstrate great potential for use in children's media production. YouTube's popularity demonstrates that there is an emerging 'clip culture' in which short video snippets of varying provenance can draw considerable viewership. The home-made and the professional sit side by side in an enormous database of clips that are not tied to a broadcast schedule but are instead at the command of the individual viewer's preference or whimsy. Amateur production has an important distribution mechanism in such social networking sites and services. Mobile phones too, in combination with computers, have proven to be powerful production and distribution platforms for similarly small-scale productions. pixel.play, an initiative of Australian Network for Art and Technology (ANAT), has been delivering mobile phone production workshops around South Australia in the past few years to considerable popular and critical success (http://www.anat.org.au/pixel.play).

Whatever the given media practices are, there are ways to capitalize on the creativity of media play and extend the pleasure of play through media production. Linking production to consumption, using computers to facilitate creative activities, and maintaining the emphasis on public and social uses of media are all ways in which after-school care services can take advantage of their unique position as media-rich intermediary spaces for children's recreation and learning.

Rather than perceiving OSHC as a battleground for popular culture wars, where combatants struggle to gain authority over *Harry Potter* and other high-appeal media properties, OSHC is more productively viewed as an intermediary space that provides unique opportunities for informal learning and which links family life with public life for children as they gain autonomy and become responsible participants in media cultures.

Appendix 1

Letter to the Parent

THE FLINDERS UNIVERSITY
OF SOUTH AUSTRALIA

Karen Orr Vered, Ph.D.
Address

Contact Details

SCREEN STUDIES
School of Humanities
Faculty of Education, Humanities,
Law & Theology

[date]

Dear Parent and Child,

This letter is written to your family because you are participants in an Out of School Hours Care program. Let me introduce myself. I am Dr. Karen Orr Vered, a lecturer of Screen Studies at Flinders University. In addition to my teaching at Uni, I also research and write about children's media. For the last year, I have been studying the use of media in Out of School Hours Care. Your OSHC service has been selected and agreed to participate in this pilot study. This is an opportunity for children to participate in a fun and important project so I hope you will join us.

Out of School Hours Care is the least studied sector of the growing child-care industry. Your involvement in this project will help establish guidelines for continued quality in care of primary school children. The research project aims to find out how television, video and computer games, and other electronic media are used in Out of School Hours Care. More importantly for you, the project is concerned with how children feel about their media use, what they value, what gives them pleasure, and how they manage their own media consumption in their leisure-time.

The project will involve observation of the children, staff, and facility approximately two or three times per week over the next six months. I will also interview the children and staff about their media use. (This is the part that kids like best.) At times, these interviews will be recorded on audio tape and occasionally on video tape. The video taped sessions will be used to present the research at national and international conferences on children's media. The audio tapes are for note keeping purposes, so that when I write reports, articles, papers, or books, I can accurately quote children's remarks and insights. If you would like to review any video tape of your child before it is presented at a conference, I can easily arrange for a preview screening. I will also take photographs from time to time. If you object to your child being photographed or video taped, please indicate this in the permission form attached. I may be able to include your child in the study without his/her photograph if you agree.

Identity of children and staff will be maintained by the standard use of pseudonyms. Children can select their own "fake name" to use in the study. The program sites will be written about as "Site A" and so forth.

This project has been approved by the Flinders University Ethics Committee, the Department of Education, Training, and Employment, and the Out of School Hours Care Association. of South Australia. If you agree to your child's participation in this project, please turn over this letter and fill-in the details on the consent form. Leave the form with OSHC staff and I will collect them. If you need further information or have any questions, please contact me on [phone], or send me an email: [address].

Thank you for considering this request. I and my research assistant, Danny Wattin, look forward to your child's participation.

Karen Orr Vered, Ph.D.
Screen Studies
Flinders University

Consent Form

I ————————————————— hereby consent to my child's involvement
    (parent/guardian name)

in the research project entitled: Recreational Media Use in Out of School
Hours Care: Case Studies in Context.

I have read and understand the Information on the above named project.
I understand my child will be observed, interviewed, and that these
sessions may be recorded on video or audio tape.

I understand that there is no payment for my child's participation in
this project.

I understand that while information obtained in this study may be published, my child will not be identified and all individual information
will remain confidential.

I understand that I may withdraw my child from the study at any stage
during the research.

I am aware that I should retain copies of the Information Sheet and
Consent Form for future reference.

I consent to ————————————————— being involved in this project.
              (child's name)

Signed ————————————————   Date————————————

Relationship to Child ——————————————————

Name of Child ——————————————————

Appendix 2

Kid's Interview Form

Interview Date   Child's Age

Child's Real Name   Pretend Name
Years at OSHC   Year in School

HOME MEDIA INVENTORY (circle & identify type where appropriate)

TV   VCR   Video Games   Computer   Internet   Game boy

ABOUT TV & VIDEO

At OSHC, do you ...

Watch TV?
Which programs?

At home, do you ...

Watch TV?
Which programs?

At OSHC, do you ...

Watch Videos?
Which ones?

At home, do you ...

Watch Videos?
Which ones?

Do you watch TV or videos in your classroom at school?

Which ones?

Are the rules the same at home, OSHC, and school? How are they different?

ABOUT VIDEO GAMES

At OSHC, do you ...

Play Video Games?
Which ones?

Why do you like these? What do you like about these games?

When you play these games at OSHC, do you play ...

Alone   w/Friend   In a Group

At home, do you ...

Play Video Games?
Which ones?

Who do you play video games with at home?

Alone   w/Friend   w/Sibling   w/Parent   In Group

Do you play Game boy at home?

Do you play Game boy at OSHC?

Do you play Game boy in your classroom or at recess/lunch?

When you play Game boy, do you play ...

Alone   w/Friend   w/Sibling   w/Parent   In Group

Are the rules the same at home, OSHC, and school? How are they different?

ABOUT COMPUTER USE

At OSHC, do you ...

Use the Computer?

What do you do on the computer? (Games, homework, write stories, draw pictures ...)

At OSHC do you use the Computer ...

Alone   w/Friend   In a Group

At home, do you ...

Use the Computer?

What do you do on the computer? (Games, homework, write stories, draw pictures ...)

At home do you use the Computer ...

Alone   w/Friend   w/Sibling   w/Parent   In Group

At school, do you use the computer ...

Alone   w/Friend   In Group

Where, in your classroom or the computer room?

What do you do on the computer at school? (get to discussion of pleasures/preferences)

Are the rules the same at home, OSHC, and school? How are they different?

Notes

Introduction

1. Details of the guidelines for classification are discussed in greater detail in Chapter 4. This research was conducted between 2000 and 2002, prior to the last revision of the guidelines and thus the comments here reflect the advice in place at the time. The OFLC website can be found at http://www.oflc.gov.au.

1 Informal Learning and Media in After-School Care

1. The State government office operated at the time of research (2000–2) as the Department of Education, Training and Employment (DETE), which included Children's Services, having responsibility for OSHC policy and administration. In mid-2002, the office was renamed as Department of Education and Children's Services (DECS), to better reflect its purview. Along with the name change, responsibilities for employment and post-secondary education were reassigned to separate ministerial supervision.
2. The OFLC has subsequently revised their guidelines, and the PG classification no longer carries the disclaimer that material will not be harmful or disturbing. Classification has become more conservative in recent years, unfortunately.
3. In Melbourne, Victoria, however, the books have been banned from several Seventh Day Adventist schools, no doubt for their themes of the occult. 'Vic: Harry Potter's witchcraft banned by Melbourne school,' AAP General News, 23 November 2001, sourced from Electronic Library Australia, 9 January 2002.
4. I need to distinguish my use of the phrase 'third place' from that of geographer Ray Oldenberg who is often associated with the concept. In *The Great Good Place* (1999 (1989)) Oldenberg uses the term 'third place' to describe places associated with adult and pre-adult (youth) life, but not children. He defines 'great good places' by the *absence of electronic media* and associates the decline of 'third places' in the US with the development of mass media.
5. This essay is also available among the resources provided by the Center for Media Literacy at their website, www.medialit.org/reading_room/article2.html.

2 Childhood and Childcare in Australia

1. For a broad yet detailed view of Australian childhood, see Jan Kociumbas's *Australian Childhood: A History* (Sydney: Allen & Unwin, 1997).
2. I am grateful to Liz Fraser from the Commonwealth Department of Family and Community Services (FACS) for providing me with a chronology of key points in the history of childcare and similar services in Australia.
3. Here Sweeney is defining the middle class by their wealth as a result of employment, whereas in earlier times, the middle-class woman would not

have worked outside the home for a wage. Nevertheless it is the overall wealth that seems to mark the middle class, whether that is acquired through one or two incomes.

4. 'Voter Guide, September 2002,' EdSource, www.edsource.org accessed 9 October 2003.

5. For more on US after-school care and its association with low-income families, see Robert Halpern *Making Play Work: The Promise of After-School Programs for Low-Income Children* (New York: Teachers College Press, 2003).

6. It is important to note that Aries derives his history of childhood from a study of representations of childhood. So while we cannot assert conclusively that images of children and their childhoods correspond to their lived realities, we can argue that the idea of such children and childhoods had to exist in order for them to be depicted. This approach to Aries's evidence is similar to an anthropological theory that explains the cave paintings of Lescaux. The depiction of certain animals in the cave paintings does not necessarily mean that these animals were 'good to eat.' The paintings may indicate that animals were 'good to think' about.

7. The sequence of Federal leadership throughout this period began with the Whitlam Labor Government from 1972 to 1975, followed by Fraser's Liberal-National Country coalition from 1975 to 1983. In 1983 the Hawke Labor Government was elected, followed by Keating's Labor Government in 1991. The 13-year Labor run ended in 1996 when John Howard's Liberal Coalition Government came to power. As this book goes to press Australian voters have just elected a Labor government who has promised childcare reform but the details are still to be revealed.

8. My gratitude to Sean Griffin for bringing this question to my attention at an early stage in the research when I gave presentations at Southern Methodist University and University of North Texas in 2001.

3   Intermediary Space

1. Across Australia primary schooling varies from state to state. Schooling is mandatory from the age of six and, in South Australia, usually begins with Reception, the intake year. Children may enter Reception at the age of five but do not have to begin until six. Some children attend Reception for a full year and others for only half a year. In all states, primary school includes an intake year (not always called Reception) through Grade Six, and in some states this extends to Grade Eight. OSHC is conceived in South Australia as childcare for school-aged children, 5- to 12-year-olds.

4   Pokemon on the Playground

1. Thomas is a make-believe name that the child selected for himself at the time of interview. To maintain the anonymity of children as required by the ethics committees of both Flinders University and DETE, children's real names are withheld and the OSHC sites are not identified explicitly. Thomas attends an inner-city school that caters to children of non-English-speaking backgrounds but Thomas's family is of Anglo descent.

2. While some people believe that restricting food advertisement will have an effect on obesity rates, to date there is no evidence to support this view. Sweden and Quebec prohibit food advertising to children, but childhood obesity rates in Sweden are similar to those in the UK and Quebec children are on par with the rest of Canada where such restrictions are not in place. (BBC News, http://news.bbc.co.uk/2/hi/health/3586585.stm). The media play v. physical play debate is discussed further in Chapter 5.

6 TV and Video in OSHC

1. Although one could argue that a lack of distinction between video games and television is also supported by the fact that video game graphics and concepts are increasingly more realistic, especially in sports genre games. For instance XBox games, such as 'FIFA 2004' and 'Tiger Woods Golf,' look and sound like television broadcasts of the sporting events that they are based upon. Important here is the fact that these games were not available when the research was conducted and the newer platforms, like XBox, were not in use at the OSHC services and none of the children mentioned these platforms in their home media inventories. Therefore, it is unlikely that these more recent developments provided any background for their comments.

7 Digital Games and the Internet in OSHC

1. 'Dobbing in' is the Australian colloquialism for what Americans would know as 'tattle telling,' 'snitching,' or 'ratting out.'

8 Making Media

1. Hollywood is less a place than it is a system of production and distribution. My intention is to highlight the commercial and populist qualities that have come to be associated with 'blockbuster movies' and not a particular national cinema.
2. Dramatic arts are strongly supported in South Australian schooling, and the state is known for its commitment to the performing arts. Every other year the capital city, Adelaide, hosts the Adelaide Festival and the Fringe Festival in which local, national, and international performances are showcased over a two-week period. Adelaide is also a sister city to Edinburgh, Scotland.
3. Although I have quoted here more extensively from boys than from girls, the girls contributed actively to this discussion. In these sessions the boys often stood up, moved about, and punctuated their remarks with bodily actions. The girls stayed seated on the floor, which may have limited their vocal projection, and they often commented to the person seated next to them rather than to the larger group.

Bibliography

'2002 Census of Child Care Services,' Department of Family and Community Services, Canberra: Commonwealth of Australia, 2003, www.facs.gov.au.

ABS (Australian Bureau of Statistics) Report 4901.0. 'Children's Participation in Cultural and Leisure Activities – South Australia, 2006,' www.abs.gov.au.

ABS Report 4402.0. 'Child Care, Australia,' www.abs.gov.au, 2002.

American Institutes for Research. 'Navigating the Children's Media Landscape: A Parent's and Caregiver's Guide,' Washington DC: Cable in the Classroom and National PTA, 2004.

Australian Broadcasting Authority. 'Kidsonline@home: Internet Use in Australian Homes,' Sydney: ABA and NetAlert, 2005.

Aries, P. *Centuries of Childhood: A Social History of Family Life*, Trans. Robert Baldick (New York: Vintage Books, 1962).

Baker, S. L. 'Rock on, Baby!: Pre-Teen Girls and Popular Music,' *Continuum: Journal of Media and Cultural Studies*, vol. 15, no. 3, 2001: 359–71.

—— 'It's Not about Candy: Music, Sexiness and Girls' Serious Play in After School Care,' *International Journal of Cultural Studies*, vol. 7, no. 2, 2004a: 197–212.

—— 'Pop in(to) the Bedroom: Popular Music in Pre-Teen Girls' Bedroom Culture,' *European Journal of Cultural Studies*, vol. 7, no. 1, 2004b: 75–93.

Bender, J., C. H. Flatter, and J. M. Sorrentino. *Half a Childhood: Quality Programs for Out-of-School Hours, Second Edition* (Nashville, TN: School Age Notes, 2000).

Bignell, J. '"Get Ready for Action!" Reading Action Man Toys,' in *A Necessary Fantasy? The Heroic Figure in Children's Popular Culture*, Jones, Dudley, and Tony Watkins, eds (New York: Garland Publishing, Inc., 2000: 231–50).

Brennan, D. *The Politics of Australian Child Care: Philanthropy to Feminism and Beyond* (Cambridge: Cambridge University Press, 1998).

Brennan, D. and C. O'Donnell. *Caring for Australia's Children: Political and Industrial Issues in Child Care* (Sydney: Allen & Unwin, 1986).

Buckingham, D. *Media Education: Literacy, Learning and Contemporary Culture* (Cambridge: Polity, 2003).

—— *After the Death of Childhood: Growing up in the Age of Electronic Media* (Cambridge: Polity Press, 2000).

Buckingham, D., J. Grahame, and J. Sefton-Green. *Making Media: Practical Production in Media Education* (London: English and Media Centre, 1995).

Buckingham, D. and J. Sefton-Green, 'Gotta catch em all: Structure, Agency and Pedagogy in Children's Media Culture,' *Media, Culture & Society*, vol. 25, no. 3, 2003: 379–99.

California Department of Education, 'California 21st Century Community Learning Centers,' www.cde.ca.gov/afterschool/21/cover.htm, accessed 9 October 2003.

'Cards craze leads to stabbing,' *The Advertiser* (Adelaide, Australia) 29 October 1999, p. 30.

Carnegie Council of Adolescent Development, 'Great Transitions: Preparing Adolescents for a New Century,' http://www.carnegie.org/sub/pubs/reports/great_transitions/gr_chpt7.html, 1995.

Considine, D. M. 'Media Literacy across the Curriculum,' 2002, p. 25. Center for Media Literacy, http://www.medialit.org/reading_room/article551.html, accessed 15 September 2005.

Damousi, J. *Depraved and Disorderly: Female Convicts, Sexuality and Gender in Colonial Austarlia* (Cambridge: Cambridge University Press, 1997).

Department of Education, Training and Employment. *Annual Report 1999*, Adelaide, Australia, 1999.

—— Administrative and Instructional Guidelines, Section Three, Part III, Division 3: Welfare of Students, Videotape Viewing, item 94, accessed 10 January 2002.

'Forgotten Ones: Girls and Boys DON'T Come out to Play,' *Network News*, Network of Community Activities, NSW, September 1993.

Fusco, D. *When School is Not Enough: A Video Documentary of the Role of Afterschool Programs in New York City* (New York: Educational Video Center, 2003).

Gailey, C. W. 'Mediated Messages: Gender, Class, and Cosmos in Home Video Games,' *Journal of Popular Culture*, vol. 27, no. 1, 1993: 81–94.

Gauntlett, D. 'Ten Things Wrong with the "Effects Model,"' in *Approaches to Audiences – A Reader*, R. Dickinson, R. Harindranath, and O. Linne, eds (London: Arnold, 1998: 120–30).

Giacquinta, J. B., J. Bauer, and J. E. Levin. *Beyond Technology's Promise: An Examination of Children's Educational Computing at Home* (London: Cambridge University Press, 1993).

Halpern, R. *Making Play Work: The Promise of After-School Programs for Low-Income Children* (New York: Teachers College Press, 2003).

Hearings and Testimony, May 13, 2003, Labor HHS Subcommittee Hearing: Statement of Arnold Schwartzenegger, p. 2. www.senate.gov, accessed 10 October 2003.

'Helping Children Become the Best They Can Be,' *wellplan*, no. 3, April 2003, p. 5.

Higman, B. W. *Domestic Service in Australia* (Melbourne: Melbourne University Press, 2002).

Hobbs, R. 'The Seven Great Debates in the Media Literacy Movement,' *Journal of Communication*, vol. 48, no. 1, 1998: 16–32.

Hodge, R. and Tripp, D. *Children and Television: A Semiotic Approach* (Stanford, CA: Stanford University Press, 1986).

Holiday Fun: Vacation Care for Children (instructional video) 1996. Network of Community Activities, Surrey Hills, NSW. Network Archive reference number, AV182.

Holloway, S. L. and G. Valentine. '"It's only as stupid as you are": Children's and Adults' Negotiation of ICT Competence at Home and at School,' *Social and Cultural Geography*, vol. 2, no. 1, 2001a: 25–42.

—— '"Technophobia": Parents' and Children's Fears about Information and Communication Technologies and the Transformation of Culture and Society' in *Children, Technology and Culture: The Impacts of Technologies in Children's Everyday Lives*, I. Hutchby and J. Moran-Ellis, eds (London: Routledge/Falmer, 2001b, pp. 58–77).

Hull, G. and J. G. Greeno. 'Identity and Agency in Nonschool and School worlds,' in *Learning in Places: The Informal Education Reader*, Z. Bekerman, N. C. Burbules, D. Silberman Keller, eds (New York: Peter Lang, 2006: 77–98).

Hutchby, I. and J. Moran-Ellis, eds. *Children, Technology and Culture: The Impacts of Technologies in Children's Everyday Lives* (London: Routledge/Falmer, 2001).

James, A., Jenks, C. and Prout, A. *Theorizing Childhood* (New York: Teachers College Press, 1998).

Jenvey, V. B. 'The Relationship between Television Viewing and Obesity in Young Children: A Review of Existing Explanations,' *Early Child Development and Care*, vol. 177, no. 8, 2007: 809–20.

Jones, D. and T. Watkins, eds. *A Necessary Fantasy? The Heroic Figure in Children's Popular Culture* (New York: Garland Publishing, Inc., 2000).

Kapur, J. 'Out of Control: Television and the Transformation of Childhood in Late Capitalism,' in *Kids' Media Culture*, M. Kinder, ed. (Durham, NC: Duke University Press, 1999: 122–36).

Kenway, J. and E. Bullen. *Consuming Children: Education-Entertainment-Advertising* (Buckingham, UK: Open University Press, 2001).

Kinder, M. *Playing with Power in Movies, Television, and Video Games* (Berkeley, CA: University of California Press, 1991).

Kline, S. *Out of the Garden: Toys and Children's Culture in the Age of TV Marketing* (London: Verso, 1993).

Kociumbas, J. *Australian Childhood: A History* (Sydney: Allen & Unwin, 1997).

Lee, N. 'The Extensions of Childhood,' in *Children, Technology and Culture: The Impacts of Technologies in Children's Everyday Lives*, I. Hutchby, and J. Moran-Ellis, eds (London: Routledge/Falmer, 2001: 153–169).

Lefebvre, H. *The Production of Space*, Trans. Donald Nicholson-Smith (London: Blackwell, 1991 (1974)).

Linderoth, J., A. Lantz-Andersson, B. Lindstrom. 'Electronic Exaggerations and Virtual Worries: Mapping Research of Computer Games Relevant to the Understanding of Children's Game Play,' *Contemporary Issues in Early Childhood*, vol. 3, no. 2, 2002: 226–50.

Livingstone, D. W. 'Informal Learning: Conceptual Distinctions and Preliminary Findings,' in *Learning in Places: The Informal Education Reader*, Z. Bekerman, N. C. Burbules, and D. Silberman-Keller, eds (New York: Peter Lang, 2006: 203–27).

Livingstone, S. M. and M. Bovill, eds. *Children and Their Changing Media Environment: A European Comparative Study* (Mahwah, NJ: L. Erlbaum Associates, 2001).

Luke, C. *Constructing the Child Viewer: A History of the American Discourse on Television and Children, 1950–1990* (New York: Praeger, 1990).

MacDougall, C., W. Schiller, and P. Darbyshire. 'We Have to Live in the Future,' in *Early Child Development and Care*, vol. 174, no. 4, 2004: 369–87.

Mackinnon, A. 'Educating the Mothers of the Nation: The Advanced School for Girls, Adelaide,' in *Worth Her Salt: Women at Work in Australia*, M. Bevege, M. James, and C. Shute, eds (Sydney: Hale & Iremonger, 1982: 62–71).

McCarthy, A. *Ambient Television: Visual Culture and Public Space* (Durham, NC: Duke UP, 2001).

—— 'The Front Row is for Scotch Drinkers,' in *Television: The Critical View, Sixth Edition*, H. Newcomb, ed. (New York: Oxford University Press, 2000: 451–69).

Mayall, B. 'Children and Childhood,' in *Critical Issues in Social Research*, S. Hood, B. Mayall and S. Oliver, eds (UK: Open University Press, 1999).

Meredyth, D., N. Russell, L. Blackwood, J. Thomas and P. Wise. *Real Time: Computers, Change and Schooling* (Brisbane: Australian Key Centre for Cultural and Media Policy, 1999).

Merlock Jackson, K. *Images of Children in American Film: A Sociocultural Analysis* (Metuchen, NJ: The Scarecrow Press, Inc., 1986).

Messenger Davies, M. *Television is Good for Your Kids* (London: Hilary Shipman Ltd., (1989), Second Edn 2001).

Mitchell, S. *Daily Life in Victorian England* (Westport, CN: Greenwood Press, 1996).

Mullan, B. *Consuming Television: Television and Its Audience* (Oxford: Blackwell Publishers Ltd., 1997).

Nikken, P. and J. Jansz. 'Parental Mediation of Children's Videogame Playing: A Comparison of the Reports by Parents and Children,' *Learning, Media & Technologies*, vol. 31, no. 2, June 2006: 181–202.

Nocon, H. and M. Cole. 'School's Invasion of "After-school,"' in *Learning in Places: The Informal Education Reader*, Z. Bekerman, N. C. Burbules, and D. Silberman-Keller, eds (New York: Peter Lang, 2006: 99–121).

Office of Film and Literature Classification, Guidelines for the Classification of Films and Videotapes (Amendment No. 3), 2000.

—— 'Computer Games and Australians Today,' Canberra: 1999.

Oldenburg, R. *The Great Good Place: Cafes, Coffee Shops, Bookstores, Bars, Hair Salons, and Other Hangouts at the Heart of a Community* (New York: Marlowe & Co., (1989) 1999).

Palmer, P. 'The Social Nature of Children's Television Viewing,' in *Television and Its Audience*, P. Drummond and R. Paterson, eds (London: BFI Publishing, 1986: 139–53).

Parker, S. *The Sociology of Leisure* (London: George Allen & Unwin Ltd., 1976).

Reiger, K. M. *The Disenchantment of the Home: Modernizing the Australian Family 1880–1940* (Melbourne: Oxford University Press, 1985).

Rogow, F. 'The "ABCs" of Media Literacy: What Can Pre-Schoolers Learn?,' http://www.medialit.org/reading_room/article566.html, originally in *Telemedium: The Journal of Media Literacy*, Spring 2002.

Schugurensky, D. 'This is Our School of Citizenship: Informal Learning in Local Democracy,' in *Learning in Places: The Informal Education Reader*, Z. Bekerman, N. C. Burbules, and D. Silberman-Keller, eds (New York: Peter Lang, 2006: 163–82).

Scott, D. and S. Swain. *Confronting Cruelty: Historical Perspectives on Child Abuse* (Melbourne: Melbourne University Press, 2002).

Sefton-Green, J. 'Informal Learning: Substance or Style?,' *Teaching Education*, vol. 14, no. 1, 2003: 37–51.

Seiter, E. *Sold Separately: Parents and Children in Consumer Culture* (New Jersey: Rutgers University Press, 1995).

—— 'Power Rangers at Preschool: Negotiating Media in Child Care Settings,' in *Kids' Media Culture*, M. Kinder, ed. (Durham, NC: Duke University Press, 1999).

Sheldon, L. and M. Loncar, assisted by G. Ramsay. *Kids Talk TV: 'super wickid' or 'dum'* (Canberra: Commonwealth of Australia, 1996).

Smith, F. and J. Barker. 'School's Out? Out of School Clubs at the Boundary of Home and School,' in *Children, Home and School: Autonomy, Connection or Regulation?*, R. Edwards, ed. (London: Falmer Press, 2002).

—— 'Contested Spaces: Children's Experiences of Out of School Care in England and Wales,' *Childhood*, vol. 7, no. 3, 2000: 315–33.

Spigel, L. *Make Room for TV* (Chicago: University of Chicago Press, 1992).

Suss, D., A. Suoninen, G. Garitaonandia, P. Juaristi, R. Koikkalainen, and J. A. Oleaga. 'Media Childhood in Three European Countries,' in *Children, Technology and Culture: The Impacts of Technologies in Children's Everyday Lives*, I. Hutchby and J. Moran-Ellis, eds (London: Routledge/Falmer, 2001: 28–41).

Sutton-Smith, B. *The Ambiguity of Play* (Cambridge, MA: Harvard University Press, 1997).

—— *Toys as Culture* (New York: Gardner Press, 1986).

—— ed. *Play and Learning* (New York: Gardner Press, Inc., 1979).

Sweeney, T. 'Inequalities in Our Provisions for Young Children,' in *Australian Welfare: Historical Sociology*, Richard Kennedy, ed. (Melbourne: Macmillan Company of Australia Pty. Ltd., 1989: 304–28).

US Department of Health and Human Services, Administration for Children and Families, Child Care Bureau. 'Linking and Learning: Lessons for Afterschool from Early Childhood System Building Efforts,' 2006.

Van Krieken, R. *Children and the State: Social Control and the Formation of Australian Child Welfare* (Sydney: Allen & Unwin, 1991).

Vered, K. O. 'Intermediary Space and Media Competency: Children's Media Play in Out of School Hours Care,' *Simile: Studies in Media and Information Literacy Education*, vol. 1, no. 2 (May) 2001, http://www.utpjournals.com/jour.ihtml?lp=simile/issue2/vered1.html.

—— 'Beyond Barbie: Fashioning a Market in Interactive Games for Girls,' in *Millennium Girls: Today's Girls around the World*, S. Inness, ed. (New York: Roman & Littlefield, 1998a: 169–91).

—— 'Blue Room Boys Play Incredible Machine; Girls Play Hopscotch: Recess, Computers, and Gender in Third Grade,' in *Digital Diversions: Youth Culture in the Age of Multimedia*, J. Sefton-Green, ed. (London: University College London, 1998b: 43–61).

'Vic: Harry Potter's Witchcraft Banned by Melbourne School,' AAP General News, 23 November 2001. Sourced from Electronic Library Australia, 9 January 2002.

'Voter Guide, September 2002,' EdSource, www.edsource.org, accessed 9 October 2003.

'What Works: Components of Exemplary After-School Programs,' in *Safe and Smart: Making After-School Hours Work for Kids – June 1998*, www.ed.gov/pubs/SafeandSmart/chapter2.html, accessed 9 October 2003.

Zelizer, V. A. *Pricing the Priceless Child: The Changing Social Value of Children* (New York: Basic Books, Inc., Publishers, 1985).

Websites

ACM (Association for Computing Machinery), www.acm.org

Australian Bureau of Statistics, www.abs.gov.au

Australian Communication and Media Authority, www.acma.gov.au

Australian Commonwealth Department of Family and Community Services, www.facs.gov.au

Australian Network for Art and Technology (ANAT), www.anat.org.au
California Department of Education, www.cde.ca.gov
Center for Media Literacy, www.medialit.org
CHI-Kids, http://sigchi.org/kids/chi-kids.html
Department of Education and Children's Services (DECS) South Australia, www.decs.sa.gov.au
HCI Bibliography, www.hcibib.org
Kaiser Family Foundation, www.kff.org
National Institute on Out-of-School-Time, www.niost.org
Office of Flim and Literature Classification, www.oflc.gov.au
Squeak, www.squeak.org

Index